MONEY MECHANICS

ENGINEER YOUR MONEY USING THE LOW RISK
DEBT & INVESTING SECRETS OF THE RICH

SARAH POYNTON-RYAN

authors
AND CO.

To Ella, Iris, Blossom, Jake, William and Joseph, may your pockets always be deep and your debts few. I encourage you to dare to dream big and fearlessly bring those ideas to life. I hope that money will be your unwavering ally, greasing the wheels for you to do or be whatever inspires you. Love you. Aunty Sarah xxx

CONTENTS

Foreword 7
A Little Disclaimer Before We Get Going 10
Introduction 13

1. From Bartering To Bitcoin: A Journey Through
   Monetary History 21
2. Breaking The Money Myth: Reassessing Assets and
   Liabilities 33
3. Money And Memories: How Our Past Shapes Our
   Financial Future 45
4. Decoding Debt: Strategies For Financial Recovery 69
5. Brick By Brick: Creating Wealth Through Property
   Investment 94
6. Share The Wealth: Understanding Stocks & Shares
   As An Investment Option 131
7. A Wealth Of Options: Navigating ETFs, Mutual and
   Index Funds 150
8. Compound Interest: The Silent Giant Of Wealth
   Accumulation 160
9. Beyond the Balance: Leveraging Credit Rewards for
   More Mileage 175
10. The Fuck You Money Fund: Your Path To
    Uncompromised Freedom 186
11. Dare To Dare: Understanding And Mitigating
    Investment Uncertainty 195
12. Diversified Pathways: Navigating the Terrain of
    Alternative Investments 206
13. Financial Leverage: Risky Business Or Winning
    Strategy? 214
14. Redefining Wealth: Turning Financial Literacy Into
    Action 222

FOREWORD

In a world filled with noise and an overwhelming amount of information, it can be challenging to discern who or what to trust when it comes to matters of money, investing, and financial independence. The pursuit of these goals is often hindered by a lack of knowledge, preventing individuals from reaching their full potential in both life and business. Unfortunately, many self-proclaimed experts, authors, and speakers make bold claims only to leave aspiring entrepreneurs bewildered and unsure about which path to follow.

Personally, I have had the privilege of dedicating my life to understanding the intricacies of business, money, and investing. Throughout my journey, I have encountered countless books, coaches, and speakers who promised the world but failed to deliver on their commitments, leaving behind a trail of disappointed individuals searching for genuine guidance.

Sarah Poynton-Ryan is the refreshing exception. Sarah is not only the real deal but also possesses an authenticity and genuine passion for helping others succeed. Her profound understanding of complex financial and investing strategies impressed me when I had the opportunity to meet her and work together during several business retreats in the UK and abroad. Sarah possesses a remarkable ability to simplify intricate concepts, making them accessible to individuals at any knowledge level. Her extensive experience in business, property, and general investing has repeatedly demonstrated outstanding returns for both her own portfolio and the mentees she guides and coaches.

Within the pages of "Money Mechanics," you will discover the simple keys employed by the top 1% to create generational wealth. Sarah unveils the secrets behind leveraging, investing, debt management, and money management strategies utilised by the elite. The beauty of this book lies in Sarah's talent for breaking down these concepts into easily understandable steps, ensuring that regardless of where you currently stand on your business or investing journey, you will be able to take action and apply these principles for your own super success.

Gone are the days of blindly following self-proclaimed gurus who offer empty promises. With "Money Mechanics," you have a trusted guide, a mentor who has been there and done it all. Sarah Poynton-Ryan's expertise and proven track record will empower you to overcome financial obstacles and engineer your money to achieve the life you desire.

Prepare to embark on a transformative journey of financial enlightenment. As you turn the pages of this book, be open to absorbing the wisdom within and applying it to your own circumstances. By embracing the knowledge shared by Sarah, you are taking a significant step towards securing your financial independence and unlocking the doors to a future filled with prosperity and abundance.

Remember, in this vast sea of information, it's crucial to align yourself with those who have walked the talk, those who have not only achieved success but also possess the genuine desire to guide others towards it. Sarah Poynton-Ryan is one of those rare gems, and "Money Mechanics" is your compass to navigate the complexities of the financial world and emerge victorious.

Let the journey begin.

Mark Wright

BBC Apprentice Winner – Forbes 30 under 30 – CEO of Wrighton Investments.

A LITTLE DISCLAIMER BEFORE WE GET GOING

Before you plunge headfirst into the ocean of "Money Mechanics", I want to just let you know that this book doesn't don a wizard's hat and it doesn't wield a crystal ball. It's not a fortune teller, and it definitely isn't your personal financial advisor. Its mission is simpler, but just as noble: to illuminate the vast landscape of financial opportunities that lies ahead for you, ripe for exploration.

The examples I share are just that - examples. They're as fictional as a money tree, designed to illustrate how certain financial instruments could, in theory, operate. This book is like a flashlight, here to shine a light on the possible, not dictate the definite.

Please, don't gloss over the "Risk" chapter. Financial success not a story where you can sneak a peek at the last page for answers. This whole book is going to give you important insights into the rollercoaster nature of investments, with all its thrilling ascents and gut-wrenching descents. We'll discuss circumstances where you might face financial setbacks and how you might pad your fall if things go south.

My aim is for you to close this book feeling empowered, ready to take the reins of your financial future. You'll be aware of the good, the bad, and the downright messy aspects of various financial paths. But remember, this book is about equipping you with the binoculars, not pointing you towards a particular horizon.

So strap in, stay curious, and enjoy the journey. Remember, when it comes to your finances, you're the captain of the ship. This book? It's merely your trusty compass, a guide to be consulted, not a mandate to be followed. Happy sailing!

INTRODUCTION

TRADING CHAINS FOR FREEDOM: AN UNCONVENTIONAL FINANCIAL AWAKENING

Did you grow up feeling like money was out of reach?

Perhaps money felt unattainable.

Perhaps the people you grew up with looked at others with money as greedy.

I remember hearing sayings like "money is the root of all evil" growing up. I heard it from family, from friends, at school, from my teachers... I never really paid attention to the meaning of statements like this or what was causing people to say them. All I knew, as a kid from a very normal working-parent family, was that despite having everything we needed, we weren't a wealthy family, and that money was something that often created stress.

The thing about money is that it matters. It matters when you don't have it. It matters when you do have it. It matters when you don't have enough and it matters when you have more than you need. It matters when you are trying to raise a family and there is childcare to pay for if you want to stay in your career. It matters when you are in a relationship that is making you unhappy but you can't afford to leave. It matters when you want to pay your bills but you can't. It matters when you need to fill your car with petrol but payday is two weeks away and you have already used your overdraft. However you perceive money, it matters.

In 2015, I was sitting in my living room surrounded by brown envelopes and letters with big red OVERDUE stamps on them. I remember sitting there with a deep sense of regret and shame, wondering how I got myself into such a mess. I hadn't even opened the brown envelopes as they were the most ominous: either council tax or, worse still, HMRC, telling me that I owed them money. At the time, I wasn't earning enough to cover all the bills and my monthly life was very much about choosing which we were going to pay because we couldn't pay everything on time. We knew that some would wait longer than others without majorly impacting us, so we were constantly playing a game of survival to keep our heads above water. I had just under £60,000 of debt - mostly expensive credit card debt - and we were just not earning enough to live and also pay back what we had borrowed.

I don't know if it was naivety, stupidity or twenty-something-year-old confidence, but in 2012, I started my first business; a photobooth hire business for weddings and events. I was a recruitment consultant at the time, and I had known for a while that my job was a job that paid me well but made me live for the weekends - the kind of job that hyped me up on payday but never made me feel excited on a Monday morning. I was always really aware that I was trading my 50-60 hours a week for a salary of £ 29,000 a year and I could never reconcile that in my mind. I always knew I wanted to work for myself but had no idea what I wanted to actually do when I grew up, let alone how to actually do it. I wasn't really qualified for anything, despite having spent three years at university. I have what they call a "drinker's degree" from Staffordshire University, UK. Honestly, I went to university so that I didn't have to get a job. I didn't go with the intention of preparing myself for life. It was in these years that my reliance on my overdraft and plastic money began.

So, eight years after I finished university, I was full of young, fearless energy and I decided to start a business. I actually advertised my photobooth before I even owned it. I took bookings and deposits for weddings the following season and it was only after I had secured the capital that I began considering how to buy the equipment. I chose a combination of savings, clients' deposits (which now I know was absolutely not the right way to do it - don't judge me, I was figuring it out) and credit cards. In my mind, I was going to buy the photo booth, and I was going to earn it all back from the business. Naively, I hadn't considered many aspects of actually running a company. I hadn't realised that being a business owner also meant knowing about marketing, staff, tax, investment, the cost of debt, customer service, budgeting, sales, logistics... the list goes on. And, not to mention, I was still employed and trying to balance work life and business life.

I launched the business and did the best I could with what I had. I made the most considered choices based on what my life had taught me up until that point about business, money, investing and debt. With hindsight, most of the choices I made weren't great. I was subsidising the company with credit cards and overdraft funds. I was paying my mortgage with company money because I didn't have my own. I wasn't putting money away for tax because no one had ever explained it to me. Looking back, it was a mess, but I didn't know what I didn't know!

I continued to live a life that was funded by the bank's money and at the time, I didn't see that this was an issue until my 0% rates ended and I couldn't get another one to balance transfer across to a new card. Up until then, all the debt I had on credit cards was always at a 0% interest rate, which meant it wasn't costing me anything to borrow it. As a twenty-something at the time, I was footloose and fancy-free. I never really thought about how I would pay it back. I assumed it would always just be 0%. No one had ever taught me that 0% credit cards are designed to bring you to a lender so that once you are there, when the special offer ends, they make their money by charging you interest on the money you have borrowed. I also didn't know (or maybe I didn't care) that the bank offering me the credit card was making money in lots of other ways from me.

No one had ever sat me down and explained debt to me. My school had never mentioned it. My parents had never mentioned it. My employers never mentioned it. And when my friends talked about credit cards, it was usually by saying "fuck it - just stick it on the plastic". Once again, don't judge me, I was young and I had a lot to learn.

Listen, I know I always had a choice and I was the one buying and paying for things on my credit cards, but in 2015, it hit me like a train. I sat there, staring at all of the papers spread out on the floor, showing huge numbers accrued by the fourteen different credit cards in my name, alongside the debt I had racked up in my business for suppliers and the overdrafts I had been living out of for three years... and I had no idea how it had got that bad.

It only took me three years to go from a young, energetic twenty-something with a bit of debt, to a stressed, financially-buckled, emotionally-broken thirty-two-year-old with a failing business and nothing but fear about how on Earth I was going to get out of the mess I had gotten myself into. It was affecting everything - my relationships, my sleep, my happiness, and my everyday life were always clouded by worrying about money. It was exhausting.

I expect you have always worked hard. I have always worked hard. My husband has always worked hard. We were a double-income household with no kids and we still couldn't balance the books. It has taken years for me to understand that, and the reason that so many of us end up like this is that, for most of us, money, debt and investing were never talked about in a positive way (or at all) as we were growing up.

Do you remember your parents seeing a guy in a red Ferrari driving past, hearing that roar of the engine and the glint of the paintwork, and hearing your parents say, "Urghh, what a dick, he must be making up for something"? I don't remember ever hearing anyone in my life say, "Wow, what an achievement, well done him, I bet he worked really hard and made great financial choices to be able to be driving that Ferrari!" Every time anyone around me saw someone who had more than we did, it was always demonised. Little did I know, this was carving out my relationship with money from a very young age.

Life for me is very different now. In 2015, I decided that living a life of debt and fear just wasn't a life I was willing to accept and I decided to begin learning about money, investing, business and debt. I started to learn about how to make money from these things and now, as I write this in 2023, my net worth is over one million pounds. I own businesses, real estate, stocks, crypto, and jewellery and I have funds that are trading in the foreign exchange markets every day. I don't tell you this to puff my chest, I tell you this because it is everything that this book is about. I have written this so that you can move away from being someone who works really hard but is forever in the red. This book is going to show you how I started small and moved from £60,000 of debt to a seven-figure net worth in under seven years. I truly believe that you can do the same if you follow the same rules!

By understanding money, investing and debt better, you will be able to move from having expensive debt or life costs that are drowning you, to a place of financial abundance through simple Money Mechanics. No longer will you have to be a slave to debt; in fact, you will be able to turn your debt into profits. You can create multiple streams of income, buy your dream home, travel the world and see your wealth grow every month. This book will help you create safety and security in your life. It will give you a sense of freedom that comes only from knowing in the back of your mind, at all times, that you can make changes to your life or do something different and regardless of whether it works or not, you will be financially ok.

In 2015, I began to surround myself with different people - people who had more money than I did - and what I learnt was that the biggest difference between me and my relationship with money, and people who had had money growing up, was that around their dinner tables with their parents and family friends, they had been surrounded by conversations about stocks, investments, businesses and leverage. Money had been talked about like it was a great thing. When compared to the "money is the root of all evil" message I was surrounded by growing up, was it any wonder that I moved towards a life where money caused me pain and stress, instead of a life where money was used as a tool to facilitate amazing things?

Money isn't everything, but it certainly helps keep the pressure off. It is ok for you to want to have money in your life. It doesn't make you greedy, it doesn't make you a bad person.

You cannot give from an empty cup. If you have nothing, you have nothing to give. Having security in your life will free you up to give time and money to others that really need it. I know, for sure, that since I have had more freedom financially, I have been able to help more people. My business gives away 1% of its turnover every year to charity. I wouldn't be able to give away anything if I didn't have that.

Money simply amplifies what is already there. If you are a good and generous, kind person then money won't change you, it will just allow you to be more of that. If you are fundamentally an arsehole then, I hate to say it, but money may well make you more of an arsehole!

Have you ever been in a situation where you couldn't leave because you couldn't afford to?

A job that you hate but pays you really well?

An abusive or loveless relationship but you don't have your own money?

A home that is too small but you don't have a month's rent, a deposit and money for a moving van to make a change?

This book will bring you the money secrets that wealthy families use so that you will never have to stay in a situation where you are unhappy or uninspired just because you can't afford to leave.

This book will help you to understand the history of money and how it really works in today's world, and to help you to know with certainty that you can have a life where you no longer have to worry about money day to day, month to month.

This book will bust some myths about wealth and how it is created, as well as allow you to understand why money is demonised and misunderstood, how the gender wealth gap has been created and why the only way to really change the trajectory of your financial future is to start engineering your money differently.

This book will show you how you can have a life where you have enough resources to feel safe, and that whatever decisions you make in your career, as a parent, as a wife or husband, in business, as an employee, or as a friend are being made because it is what you truly want and not simply what you can afford to do.

I invite you to discover the good and bad aspects of money, debt and investing.

I invite you to open your mind to more than the majority of people would have you believe about money, debt and investing so that you can change your future.

I invite you to become a Money Mechanic.

CHAPTER 1

FROM BARTERING TO BITCOIN: A JOURNEY THROUGH MONETARY HISTORY

M oney. We all have experience of it. We all know how we feel about it. But how much do you really know about it?

Money has been a defining part of human society since the dawn of civilisation. It has facilitated the exchange of goods and services, acted as a store of value and even been used as a symbol of power and prestige. Over the years, the way that money has been used, distributed and experienced has changed to reflect the economic conditions of the period.

Right now, it is easy to look at modern life and take financial freedoms for granted.

But let's be really honest, financial 'freedoms' don't come equally to everyone, do they?

There is a huge difference between the way that different genders, ethnicities and social classes experience money. Throughout history, money has been used to reinforce control and oppress, as well as to empower and support individuals and communities.

By understanding more about how society has experienced money over time, you can begin to understand why your own, personal money story exists like it does. The second you understand that your personal wealth has been influenced by the world around you, you will have all the tools you need to create financial independence in your life.

Money impacts us all every day. It impacts our children, our parents, families, work colleagues, neighbours, business partners and friends. Yet in middle and lower-income families across the world, we are not talking about how money really works enough. In fact, in many places, we are simply not talking about money at all.

Imagine a world where we are taught how to engineer our money from a young age - a world where every person has more than one income, where we all understand the basics of investing and making money work. The world would be a very different place. Implementing Money Mechanics will give you the power to use money as a tool in your favour instead of it controlling every aspect of your everyday life.

I can't remember any time as a child or young adult openly talking about money with my family or friends. I remember always being sure that it was rude to ask about money, to talk about how much things cost or to show off by buying 'flash' things. I remember hearing the message "If you show off that you have money, then someone will just try to take it from you" over and over as I was growing up. I certainly wasn't encouraged to ask questions about money and I didn't really start to properly understand how money really works until I was well into my thirties.

Openly talking about money is a privilege of the wealthy.

Talking about money, being open about it and, more importantly, understanding money is crucial for survival when you have little-to-no money. And yet the wealthy talk about money and how they can make it work for them all of the time, and lower-income people still think it's bad manners. This is the wrong way around!

The lack of conversation about money cannot continue. The fact that the majority of people are completely unaware of just how simple it is to engineer their money to take the pressure off and create a life in which they can thrive blows my mind. I was one of those people until recently, but when I started to include money in my everyday conversations, my life changed.

I remember when I was about twenty-two, I asked someone in my office about what they were earning in front of my boss. I was called into the office for a meeting and told that it was unprofessional to ask colleagues about how much they earned and that I needed to "learn to be more discreet". Because we have been misled to believe that we shouldn't be talking about money, we now have giant wealth gaps and increased debt on a global scale.

Let me hit you with a few figures that I discovered when I was researching this chapter.

According to The Money Charity Statistics Archive, in April 2023, the average total debt per UK household was £65,510, including mortgages.

Did you know that the UK's total personal debt, according to the same archive, in February 2023 was £1,839,300,000,000?

If you are anything like me and that is way too many zeros for you to get your head around, that is £1,839.3 billion. A figure that has increased since December 2021 by a whopping £72.3 billion.

And no one is talking about money! Because it is considered rude? WTF?

Here is something else that will blow your mind. The interest payments that were paid by UK households in 2022 were £55,803 million, an average of £153 million per day. That is money that people in debt are paying out in interest to the banks and credit card operators for the 'privilege' of being in debt.

The average savings in a UK household is £2,160 annually. However, there is a huge disparity between low-income families who only managed to save £95 in 2022 and high-income families saving £6,978 in the same 12 months.

If I told you that in the UK, the average credit card with a market typical interest rate would take twenty-five years and ten months to pay off by simply paying the minimum payment each month, starting at £61 in month one and reducing over time, would you be surprised? I was!

But imagine if you knew, like Money Mechanics do, that if you just stuck to £61 a month instead of letting the payment reduce every month, the same credit card would take five years to clear.

Of course, the banks don't want you to know this because it is how they make their money. And because we are convinced that talking openly about money is somehow a bad thing, most people never learn a better way!

Money has become a way to control the masses but money didn't start life as a representation of control. Money was simply a means of trade.

The concept of currency, as we understand it today, did not exist in the earliest human societies. Instead, people relied on barter, or the exchange of goods and services, to trade. But what they discovered fairly quickly is that it is really hard to exchange when there are no clear parameters for measuring value. For example, how many goats does it take to trade for a cow? How many bread rolls does it take to buy horseshoes from the blacksmith?

Without a standardised value measure, this was very inefficient. Over time, objects such as shells or beads were used to standardise the values, and over time these commodities developed into the creation of coins made of precious metals and stamped with images. Coins were a far more effective measure of consistent value.

The introduction of coins was useful for trading but the consequence of this convenience meant that social hierarchies began to emerge. The people who controlled the production of coins, such as kings and emperors, had the power to determine their value and often used this power to enrich themselves at the expense of others. This meant that money was often a symbol of power and prestige, rather than simply a means of exchange.

Now this is a short history lesson, I promise. It was the evolution of money that really introduced the feudal system. I am telling you this because it really does make a difference in how we all experience money today.

The feudal system was a social and economic system that existed in Mediaeval England, and it was based on a hierarchy of classes:

1. **Monarch**: The king or queen was the highest-ranking member of society and held absolute power over the land.

2. **Nobility**: The nobility was made up of lords and barons who controlled large areas of land granted to them by the monarch.

3. Knights: Knights were members of the military who were trained in combat and chivalry. They were granted land by lords and were expected to provide military service in exchange for their land.

4. Clergy: The clergy were members of the church, and they held significant power and influence in mediaeval society. They were responsible for providing spiritual guidance and were often involved in political affairs.

5. Peasantry: The peasantry was the largest class in mediaeval society, made up of serfs and freeholders. Serfs were tied to the land they worked on and were obligated to provide labour and other services to their lords. Freeholders, on the other hand, owned their own land and were responsible for their own livelihoods.

This class system was rigid and hierarchical, and it was really difficult for an individual to move up or down the social ladder. The feudal system began to decline in the late mediaeval period and it was eventually replaced by a more modern system. Even though we have a more modern system these days, there are still underlying core differences that come from the personal wealth of each layer of society.

Now you might be thinking, why does any of this matter to me? How is knowing the history of money going to help me to become more wealthy? Well, the history of money ultimately defines its future and your financial independence is intrinsically linked to how you choose to embrace its evolution.

You achieve financial independence when you have enough money to support yourself without relying on others. It is the only way to live a life of true choice. When you are financially independent you have the freedom to make choices about your life based on what you actually want.

You can choose where you live, what you do for work and how you spend your time with the peace of mind that comes from not having to live paycheck to paycheck. When you are not financially independent, you live in fear of unexpected expenses, job loss or your landlord giving you notice. The majority of people in 2023 are not financially independent. Most people rely on one, single, finite income. Inflation has shot from 2% to 10.1%, and gas and electricity costs have more than doubled, so being a Money Mechanic and engineering your finances has never been more important. Relying on a single income is too risky.

A report published in June 2022, by the Department of Work & Pensions, revealed that 64% of UK households relied on wages from employment as their main source of income, with 9% earning from self-employment, 7% from state pensions, 8% from private pensions, and only 1% from investments. A survey carried out by Beam.org discovered that UK adults could only cover their monthly bills for two and a half months if they were to lose their jobs because most people do not have any source of investment income.

These statistics are almost the same across the USA with only 62% of Americans having any kind of savings (according to a study carried out by Bankrate.com). And in France, homelessness more than doubled between 2020 and 2021, moving from 143,000 people to 300,000 in a twelve-month period. Money, and the lack of it, is the biggest contributing factor to these painful statistics.

Financial independence starts with financial literacy and this is really where understanding why your money situation is the way it is begins. What we know for sure is that the lack of financial literacy in households is what deepens inequality in today's world. History shows that wealthier households tend to have more time and resources to teach their children about money and investing. Research carried out by St James's Place found that teenagers from more affluent backgrounds scored more highly in financial literacy tests than their peers from lower-income households.

This goes even deeper when you start to look at the gender wealth gap and disparities in wealth by race and ethnicity. In the 2019 survey of consumer finances, it was found that the long-standing and substantial wealth gaps between families in different racial and ethnic groups are still vast, with white families having eight times the wealth of a typical black family and five times the wealth of a typical Hispanic family.

Globally, women are less financially independent than men. This isn't because women are not as good with money as men! And in the words of Taylor Swift, all women are sick of running as fast as they can, wondering if they would get there quicker if they were a man. The truth is that we actually do have further to run, when it comes to money.

Women have not had as many years to be independently handling their own financial affairs.

It wasn't until 1919 in the USA, and 1928 in the UK, that women were allowed to vote. There are still many parts of the world where voting rights are really difficult to enjoy. Vatican City is the last place that forbids women to vote entirely.

It was 2015 before women in Saudi Arabia were allowed to vote, and 2017 before women in Saudi Arabia were permitted to go to university or get a job without permission from their father or husband.

In the UK, it was 1975 before women were allowed to have their own bank account in their own name because they were seen as a risk by the bank, and single women were not permitted to apply for a loan or credit card in their own name without a signature from their father.

It wasn't until 1900 that women were allowed to own and control property in the USA. In the UK, it was 1922 and in India, it was 1956 before women had the same rights as men to control real estate assets.

It wasn't until 1982 that women were allowed to buy their own drink with their own money in a British pub.

Is it any wonder we have a huge gender wealth gap?

Money, investing and debt have been experienced so differently by every social group in our society. Women are years behind men when it comes to working with money, having confidence in controlling money and, crucially, being allowed to make decisions about how to put money to work.

Women are less likely to invest than men, with just 66% of women investing outside of retirement plans.

In the USA, when lower-income households do invest, they are more likely to invest in precious metals such as gold, whereas higher-income households are more likely to invest in property and real estate or companies, which generate passive income through dividends. Now, on the surface, it is great that lower-income households are investing anything, but let's break this down a bit.

Gold is a lump of shiny metal. It will not pay you anything, it does not produce anything. In some cases, holding gold actually costs money. The only way you make money from gold is if someone is willing to pay you more for the lump you own than you paid for it originally.

A property can be rented out or improved and sold at an increased value. A productive company will pay passive dividends to its shareholders. So you can make money in multiple ways with these types of investments.

Why do lower-income people choose gold instead of companies or real estate?

Because lower-income households do not have access to the same information and education and experience as higher-income households. It really is that simple! Lower-income households are being whipped into a frenzy by the news and media generally telling them that it is all doom and gloom. Whereas the wealthy are listening to the markets and their advisors and have higher levels of confidence because they are experiencing success.

Money has been central to human society for thousands of years and has played a crucial role in shaping our social, economic and cultural systems. Understanding the history of money and the ways in which different groups have experienced it over time is essential for building a more equitable and sustainable financial future for us all. As we navigate the challenges of the 21st century, it is more important than ever to recognise the ways in which money can be used to empower or oppress, and work towards a financial system that is fair, transparent and accessible to all.

The first stepping stone is the promotion of financial literacy and inclusion and policies that address systemic inequalities. We can create a world in which everyone has the opportunity to achieve financial independence and security.

But how do we shift from being one of the people that are only seventy-five days away from financial ruin to someone who has an emergency fund and enough money to make decisions because they want to and not because they can't afford to?

In a world where job security and retirement benefits are increasingly uncertain, we all have to take responsibility for our own financial well-being. This means understanding how to save, invest, and manage money. We all have to become Money Mechanics!

You will have lots of questions I know.

Should you save money or clear debt?

Should you invest if you have debt?

How much do you need to start creating additional income streams?

How do I measure risk?

Where do I start?

How do you choose where to put money?

As we move through this book, you will have the answers you need to all of these questions, and an idea of the steps you can take to become financially independent and secure.

It has never been more important for people of all ages to be striving for financial independence. It is really hard to get there, especially when you are in debt. But it is possible and you really can start with as little as £10, £50 or £100. In a modern world, where economic uncertainty is the only thing that is certain, financial independence is more important than ever.

By the end of this book you will be a Money Mechanic and a Money Mechanic knows that it doesn't matter where you start, it is where you finish that counts.

Financial abundance is something that everyone can consciously strive for. It is possible for everyone to achieve but it doesn't happen overnight. It will take some people longer than others because we are not all starting from the same place, however, I promise that if you implement what you are going to learn in this book, then you will change the trajectory of your finances forever.

Imagine a world where all people were certain about their finances. Where people had the freedom to travel more, experience more, leave relationships that were no longer serving them, follow their calling instead of staying in jobs they hate because they can't afford to leave...

Sounds pretty epic, doesn't it?

CHAPTER 2
BREAKING THE MONEY MYTH: REASSESSING ASSETS AND LIABILITIES

For as long as I can remember, I believed that if I purchased things and I owned them, then I was building wealth.

Even if I purchased something on finance (like a car), I really thought that because I would own the car once the finance was paid off, I was better off!

It simply isn't true! We have all been lied to! Just because you own something does not mean it is adding to your wealth.

Understanding the difference between an asset and a liability is the fundamental lynchpin for you to be able to achieve financial independence.

An asset puts money into your pocket, while liabilities take money out of your pocket.

Knowing how to really differentiate between the two is something that many people simply do not understand.

For years, I was taught that a car, a house, or anything I owned was an asset. I imagine, if you are reading this book, you were probably taught the same. In fact, many people reading this book will still consider their own home an asset. I know this because I posted a video about this on my TikTok in 2022 and I had hundreds of people telling me that I was wrong. They were telling me that their own home is an asset. You can head to @sarahpoynton on TikTok to find that video.

Lower-income households have been taught to believe that things we own are assets but the reality is not as black and white as that.

Assets are items that can be converted into cash or generate income over time. These may include things such as rental properties, stocks, bonds, or even small businesses. When you own true assets, those assets put you in a position to generate revenue and grow your wealth from the ownership of that asset.

A liability, on the other hand, refers to obligations that require you to pay money out now, or over an agreed time frame. These can include things such as credit card debt, car loans, or mortgage payments.

The house that you live in is not an asset, it is a liability.

That car you are driving is not an asset, it is a liability.

That student loan you have for your education isn't an asset, it is a liability.

But most people, like me, were taught the exact opposite. This is one of the main reasons that the masses stay in debt because they do not understand this important rule of creating wealth.

I know some of you will be thinking, "Sarah, you just have no idea what you are talking about", but hear me out.

This is what you really need to know:

YOUR PERSONAL RESIDENCE

Many people believe that owning a home is an asset. You live in it, it has value, you could always sell it and it may go up in value. All of that is true, in principle. However, unless the home is generating rental income, it is actually a liability because it requires you to physically pay mortgage payments out of your own personal money. Additionally, there is property tax to pay, maintenance costs to keep that house in great condition and other expenses associated with owning and living in a home.

While a personal residence may appreciate in value over time, this appreciation is usually modest, may not keep pace with inflation and is not guaranteed. Additionally, selling a home can be expensive because of legal fees and sales fees, not to mention time-consuming, with property sales in the UK taking a minimum of 4 weeks and up to 12 months in some cases. This barrier means it is hard to turn the equity in your home into liquid cash.

In many cultures, owning a home has always been considered a sign of success and stability. This is especially true in the UK and USA. People believe that owning a home is a crucial step towards achieving financial independence, but how independent are you really when you have to sign a death pledge that locks you into 35 years of debt?

Mortgage literally translated means death (mort) pledge (gage).

I was always taught that buying a house meant I had an asset, but who is really pushing the agenda of home ownership?

Estate agents

Brokers

Banks

All the people that get paid when you buy or sell your home.

We become very emotionally attached to our own homes. We see it as a source of security. When I tell you that it is a liability and not an asset, it will be hard for you to get your head around if this is the first time you are hearing this. But if you are personally paying to live there, paying all the costs to look after it, paying down the debt and covering the interest on your mortgage, then that building isn't adding to your financial independence, it is costing you money.

An asset doesn't cost you money. A liability does!

We will explore property and real estate investing in Chapter 5. For now, a shift in mindset is required. Unless the house you live in is putting money in your pocket, as realised cash flow, then it is costing you money, which makes it a liability.

Yes, you might make a profit when you sell at some point in the future. But hope is not a wealth creation strategy and there are thousands of people who are in negative equity when they come to sell. Profit isn't promised.

And have you factored in true costs? Most people haven't.

When you buy your home with a mortgage, you will pay an interest rate on the amount you borrow. In the UK, at the time of writing, that is around 4.5%. If you purchased your property for £100,000 on a thirty-five-year mortgage you would have paid roughly £473.26 per month for 420 months which is £198,796.20. Buying that property didn't cost £100,000 at all, it cost you almost double that. So unless you can sell for almost double what you paid for the house, you will not realise a profit. And I haven't mentioned the costs of the upkeep and insurance, but that will soon mount up as well.

If your property has cost you money and not made you money, then it is not an asset.

A NEW CAR

There is something very special about getting into a new car - the smell, the shine… It feels fantastic. But a car depreciates in value and costs you money to maintain. You have insurance to pay for, fuel, services, MOTs, tyres and more.

As soon as you drive your car out of the dealership, it loses a significant portion of its value and that trend will continue over time. If you sell your car (except in exceptional cases), you are likely to be paid less for it than you paid.

Well into my thirties, I used to look at people with big, fast, expensive cars and think wow, they must have loads of money. I am a sucker for a fast car, I won't lie. When I started to learn about money and debt, I realised that most people driving around in fancy cars don't actually own them. They are owned by a bank that has lent them the money to buy it. That perception of "looking rich" has only been created by having expensive debt.

Many of those people are driving around in giant bank loans, often higher than their annual salary, which is crazy when you really think about it. Society sees owning a car as a status symbol - the bigger and better the car, the more successful you must be.

But there is a difference between how low-income households and wealthy households buy cars. The wealthy know that a car is a liability. They will invest in a cash-flowing asset that creates enough money to cover the cost of the car. They don't drain their own personal resources to have the car. Lower-income households are taking out expensive debt to buy the car, and then have to maintain it and run it out of their own resources.

Do you see the difference?

Unless you are buying a car that you will use to make money, such as a taxi or a car hire company, then your car is taking money out of your pocket and so it is a liability.

Next time you feel the green-eyed monster creeping in over someone cruising by you in a sports car, just remind yourself that the idea behind financial independence is to **be** rich, not to just **look** rich!

There is a massive difference!

CREDIT CARDS

I am sure this will come as no surprise but I believe that credit cards are the devil in the wrong hands. Credit cards were my downfall until I learnt about how debt and money really worked. In 2015, I had almost £60,000 in debt. A big chunk of that was on credit cards. I know about credit cards at a very personal level.

Credit cards give you access to money. That much is true.

However, the way that rich people and poor people use credit cards is fundamentally different. If I asked you right now to tell me exactly what your interest rates were across all your credit card facilities and overdraft facilities, could you tell me with certainty?

Do you really understand that when you take out a credit card, you are taking out a loan from the provider that has interest rates and fees associated with that loan?

I understood this in theory, but when I started borrowing, I had no idea how this impacted my real-world finances. No one ever taught me how to use a credit card, I simply used to "stick it on the plastic". In my late teens and early twenties, it felt like free money. I had no plan of how to pay it back, I just figured it would all work itself out. It didn't.

In my late twenties, I wanted to start clearing the debt, but my resources were limited. I thought the best thing to do was to pay the minimum payment to get it cleared without overstretching myself. No one ever sat me down and explained to me that these loans, rolling over every month, for years at a time, are catastrophic for your financial independence. We will talk about this more in Chapter 4.

Society has been brainwashed by clever advertising, social pressure, reward programs and a lack of financial literacy, to believe credit cards are an asset, but, that totally depends on how disciplined you are when using them. When lower-income people use a credit card it drains their wealth which makes that credit card a liability.

When the wealthy use a credit card, they get access to money, they usually earn rewards points such as Avios for flights or shopping vouchers and they clear their balances monthly, so those mini-loans actually improve the users' wealth.

If a credit card is adding to your wealth, it is an asset. If your credit cards are costing you money, then they are a liability.

EXPENSIVE CLOTHING OR JEWELLERY

One of my favourite things is looking down at my wrists and seeing my favourite Cartier jewellery. Every time I see it, I am reminded of the road I have travelled to get to where I am today. I am grateful and proud of the old me for the choices she made.

I understand that it feels great to have nice things. Buying expensive things actually can make you feel amazing. Remember though, the goal is to be financially independent and have enough to not have to worry about money. The goal is not to look rich on the surface while managing crippling debt and all the stress that comes with it.

There is a fundamental difference between how the rich and poor buy clothes, jewellery and accessories. Wealthy people are more likely to invest in very specific, high-quality, timeless pieces that hold their value over time. They often buy with cash as a way of diversifying their portfolios.

Whereas, lower-income people tend to buy what is trendy and in fashion, often using credit cards that take years to pay off, all for the pleasure of instant gratification. Payment tools like Klarna have exploded into the retail market to make buying the things you want less painful upfront, but these services have huge back-end penalties if you pay late or miss a payment. If you are not good with money then these services do the opposite of helping you, they are tying you up in more debt which drains your resources

Jewellery, accessories and clothing can be an asset if acquired by focusing on high quality, an evidenced track record and informed financial decisions. If the items you buy are looked after, insured and cared for effectively, then they may well be an asset. For example, if you take a Hermes Birkin Handbag. These handbags sell from $9,000 to the most expensive one, the Sac Bijou Birkin, priced at around $2,000,000.

If I had $2,000,000 available to invest in a Birkin, I absolutely would. The Sac Bijou Birkin is beautiful and also a fantastic investment. A study that was carried out by Baghunter found a Birkin handbag to be a better investment than the S&P 500 (a stocks and shares fund we will talk about later in the book) and gold when assessed over the past thirty-five years. The study found that the stock market had a real return of 8.65% per year, gold had a real return of -1.5%, and Birkin handbags had risen 14.2% over the same period. The Hermès bag has never fluctuated downwards.

Overall though, the jewellery, accessories and clothing that most people are spending their money on are liabilities. Most people are draining their resources to buy them. Most items lose value quickly, usually faster than it takes to clear the credit card used to buy it in the first place. That makes these items liabilities and not assets.

UNIVERSITY / COLLEGE DEGREES

I have a degree and I don't regret it at all. This chapter though is about the difference between assets and liabilities. Many people decide to invest in their higher education on the assumption that the qualification will be an asset that pays dividends in the form of improved career opportunities.

While education is valuable, student loans come with high-interest rates and in reality, higher education doesn't always lead to higher-paying jobs.

Currently, in the UK, the student loan interest rate is 7.3%. In the USA, these rates go as high as 7.54% on some loans. I accept that education is important. I totally believe in the improvement of skills and knowledge, but taking on debt to finance a degree that might turn into improved wealth later on, is going to drain your resources, which makes it a liability.

In the UK, student loan debt is estimated to have surpassed £120 billion in 2021, with an average debt per student of over £40,000. According to the Office for National Statistics, the average annual tuition fee in the UK for 2019/20 was £9,188, with some courses costing significantly more.

This high cost of education can lead to significant student loan debt and ongoing financial burdens for many people, especially if the degree doesn't lead to a higher-paying job - and let's be honest, not everyone gets a higher-paying job - or even a relevant job - after they study. It is estimated by some studies that more than half of people that studied for a degree are not actually working in the field for which they studied. Most of them are still paying for that education years later. I am one of those people.

According to the Institute for Fiscal Studies, more than a third of UK graduates are working in jobs that don't require a degree. This means that these graduates are not earning a higher income than non-graduates, making the investment in their education a liability.

If you are thinking about studying, really look at what you will do with that investment of money and whether it will genuinely pay dividends in the future. Because there are so many other ways to get life experiences that do not tie you up in debt for years.

In the UK, it takes on average twenty-one years to pay off a student loan. No one explained that to me properly when I was nineteen and working out if I wanted to go to university or not. I imagine no one really explained it to you and if you have children of university/college age, I bet you haven't explained it to them either. Lower, middle and working-class people generally just follow the pack - work hard at school, go to university, get a good job, work up the ladder, pay taxes, retire at sixty-five, and live on a pension until they die. That is what we are told is a 'good life'. This doesn't compute in my head as a good life, especially now that there is so much more access to opportunities globally. A university or college degree simply is not an asset in the same way it once was.

Many things in the world have a monetary value attached to them, but that does not make them an asset. If something does not generate income, appreciate in value or contribute to building your wealth then it is a liability.

Now you understand the differences between assets and liabilities, you can build a strong financial foundation for yourself, and you can spread this message to your family, children and friends.

If all children were educated in these financial fundamentals as they are growing up, the world would be a very different place in ten, twenty, fifty, a hundred years. The only way to break the cycle of poverty is to learn how to make money, debt and investing work for you instead of against you.

ACTION: Head over to:

www.sarahpoynton.com/moneymechanicsresources where you will find a worksheet that you can use to assess your assets and liabilities. Ask yourself these questions:

1. Does it generate income?
2. Does it appreciate in value?
3. Does it require ongoing expenses?
4. Is it easy to sell quickly?

This will help you better understand where you are starting from today.

CHAPTER 3
MONEY AND MEMORIES: HOW OUR PAST SHAPES OUR FINANCIAL FUTURE

Your current financial situation is a result of all the decisions you have made with money before this moment. Your current situation is a consequence of your choices.

Hard to hear? Maybe!

True? Absolutely!

It can be extremely difficult to hear that our current financial situation is the result of our past decisions. It may not be your fault but it is always your responsibility. This realisation is empowering when you really embrace it. It puts the power to change things in your hands. You can only make improvements in the future by taking responsibility for your choices and learning from your mistakes.

You are a Money Mechanic now and we don't dwell on the past. We accept the decisions we have made up until now and we commit to making the right decisions to move towards financial independence and security.

This chapter is all about your money story; understanding it and resetting it.

In the words of Albert Einstein, Doing the same thing expecting different results is the definition of insanity!"

If you do not change anything after reading this book then nothing will change. The transaction doesn't bring the result, the activity does. Imagine buying a gym membership and expecting your jeans to fit better without stepping foot inside. Knowing what to do isn't enough. You must activate change. There is no shortcut, you simply have to do the work.

There is no magic money pill, sadly. If you started reading this book hoping that I would give you a hack that would make you super-wealthy, really quickly, without any effort, then I am going to have to let you down. But don't shred this book just yet, keep reading because the work is actually very simple, you just have to be committed to doing it.

The first step is to work out what has happened up to this point. For most of us, the financial decisions we make as adults are formed from the psychological relationship we have with money that began when we were children. That relationship is referred to as your 'money story' and it is not something you get to choose. It is carved into you as you grow up, based on what happens around you.

"I remember bailiffs coming to the door and asking if my mum was home," John said.

"I had to go to the shops and get electricity on cards for the metre so we could keep all the lights on and I was always told to buy cigarettes at the same time for my mum, back when kids were allowed to do that," Paul admitted.

"My dad went bankrupt because he didn't keep up with the mortgage payments on our house when he got divorced from my mum. He always blamed her, saying that if she hadn't left, he would have had more money," Janine told me.

"My parents never spoke about money around us. I never knew if we had enough or not. It was considered rude to talk about money in our house," Vicky shared.

"'What do they think I am, made of money?' My dad always used to say this whenever I asked to go on a school trip or extra activity with school," Donna said.

"Money doesn't grow on trees."

"Money is the root of all evil."

"Neither a borrower nor a lender be."

"Rich people are greedy."

"Never tell anyone you have money or they will try to take it from you."

"To be rich, you have to be taking from the poor."

"Money should be saved for a rainy day."

"Money won't make you happy."

"There are more important things in life than money."

"There isn't enough money to go around."

"If I have too much money, I will lose sight of my values."

"You need money to make money."

"I am not good with money."

"My family has always struggled for money."

These are just some of the statements I heard when I asked people about money when researching this book. I spoke to low-income, working and middle-class people. I asked them what their experience of money was growing up. These are all real stories and statements from real people. The general tone is pretty bleak, isn't it? I bet you have heard some of those statements haven't you?

Our personal money story forms the foundation of our attitudes and behaviours toward money. If we grew up in an environment where financial conflicts were prevalent, talking about money can trigger feelings of anxiety or discomfort. Similarly, if we were not taught about financial literacy or we experienced a lack of transparency around money, we may find it challenging to navigate the complexities of personal finance as adults. This has certainly been my own experience.

When compared to the responses I got from people that grew up wealthy, the differences are vast.

"My dad paid me an allowance based on the number of books I read. He believed that investing time and effort into personal development was the most important thing I could do and so he rewarded that behaviour with my allowance," David told me.

"My parents used to tell me often to live below my means and invest the rest," Michelle responded.

"My mum always said that if you only have one income stream then you are playing a risky game," Nyasha confessed.

"Saving money in the bank instead of investing it is like setting fire to fifty pound notes my grandad always told me," said Erin.

There are lots of really positive statements about money from famous thought leaders that many low, working and middle-class people have never heard of:

"If you want to be rich, simply serve more people,"

ROBERT KIYOSAKI

"Too many people spend money they earned, to buy things they don't want, to impress people that they don't like,"

WILL ROGERS

"Money is a terrible master but an excellent servant,"

P.T. BARNUM

"If we command our wealth, we shall be rich and free. If our wealth commands us, we are poor indeed,"

EDMUND BURKE

"We make a living by what we get, but we make a life by what we give,"

WINSTON CHURCHILL

"Never spend your money before you have it,"

THOMAS JEFFERSON

> "You must gain control over your money or the lack of it will forever control you,"

DAVE RAMSEY

> "It is not how much you earn but what you do with it that determines your end,"

OLUMIDE EMMANUEL

The difference between what we are taught about money in lower-income households vs wealthy households is apparent. These messages have influenced our mindset toward money as adults. The cycle of poverty is really hard to break away from because there is no circuit breaker to educate financial literacy in schools and offices and communities throughout the world. Take a look at the image below.

Cycle Of Poverty

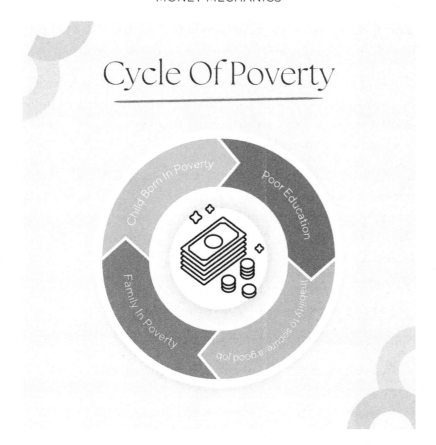

There is a book called Men At Arms, by author Sir Terry Pratchett. In this book, Pratchett introduced the Boots Theory and it perfectly explains, more eloquently than I could, the basics of why rich people stay rich and poor people stay poor. I would highly recommend taking a look at the full passage in the book. In summary, though, Sam Vimes' Boots Theory of socioeconomic unfairness boils down to the fact that wealthier people can afford to buy hardwearing boots that last a decade or more. Poorer people can only afford cheap boots that need replacing frequently with another cheap pair. At the end of the decade, the wealthy people will have paid for one, good-quality pair of boots whilst the poor people will have ultimately spent significantly more money on several pairs of cheaper boots.

If our attitudes towards money are shaped by our upbringing, and our financial capabilities determine our behaviours, as in the Boots theory, you can see why, for many of us, breaking away from poverty is so hard to do.

Everyone's relationship with money is unique and deeply personal. Our money mindset is influenced by our upbringing, our education and personal experiences. Understanding what your money story actually is, is the first step in improving your financial position.

Take a break from reading for a short time, grab yourself a cuppa and a pad and pen and sit and reflect on these things:

You can download this worksheet from:

www.sarahpoynton.com/moneymechanicsresources

1. What do you believe to be true about money?
2. Identify any negative beliefs or habits around money that may be holding you back.
3. Reflect on your upbringing and early experiences with money. What do you remember, feel, and understand?
4. Think about the words you heard about money from parents and caregivers.
5. Do you feel comfortable talking about money in your household now? If not, why not?
6. Have you experienced financial setbacks in your life? How do you think these setbacks moulded your relationship with money today?
7. What emotions do you associate with money?

8. Do you feel anxious about your finances or confident and in control?

This task of reflection is going to help to identify any limiting beliefs or negative patterns that are holding you back. It might feel uncomfortable in parts but write your truth. You can always burn it after if you don't want anyone to read it, but write your truth so that you can understand yourself better.

This level of personal awareness will empower you to start moving away from the money story that has shaped your relationship with money up until now and toward a financially independent life.

When I first heard the terms 'money mindset' and 'money story' I literally had no idea what it meant and I certainly couldn't work out what my personal style was. I didn't know what I didn't know. If you are anything like me, then this next bit will come in useful.

Here are ten typical money mindset styles and an explanation of each. I am personally a blend of a few of these money mindset styles and you may be as well.

THE SCARCITY MONEY MINDSET

Have you ever felt like you're constantly walking on eggshells when it comes to money?

That's the scarcity money mindset, my friend. It's like having a little voice in your head that constantly reminds you that money doesn't grow on trees, and you better hold onto every penny for dear life.

Growing up in a family where money was always tight can definitely leave a lasting impression on your financial beliefs and behaviours. Over sixteen million people in the UK have less than £100 in savings and so, for many people, money is directly linked to scarcity and not having enough.

It is estimated that only 39% of UK adults are saving enough for retirement, and many people are not taking advantage of workplace pension schemes. In the US, research conducted by the National Institute Of Retirement Security (NIRS) found that around 60% of American households are at risk of not having enough retirement income to maintain their pre-retirement standard of living. Being surrounded by these scenarios teaches us, from a young age, that money is scarce.

Unfortunately, a scarcity money mindset can lead to some pretty unhelpful financial habits as adults. Hoarding, overspending, and avoiding risks like the plague are the most common. It's like trying to run a marathon with a backpack full of rocks. Many people want to change but their habits, usually controlled by their subconscious mindset, sabotage any progress.

The good news is that there are ways to overcome this mindset and develop a healthier relationship with money. Think of it like switching from survival mode to thriving mode. It's not always easy, but with some simple financial education (that you are learning in this book) and some support, it's definitely possible.

Just remember, you don't have to be a financial wizard to activate change. We all start at the beginning. Taking small steps towards a better financial future is always better than standing still. The smallest adjustment can make a huge difference to a healthier money mindset and bank balance.

THE ABUNDANCE MONEY MINDSET

Usually, people with this mindset have grown up in surroundings where money was abundant, like being born into a family where money does actually grow on trees. Lucky ducks, right? They probably associate money with security and freedom.

Studies show that those with an abundance mindset tend to have a more positive and empowered relationship with money. It's like having a superhero cape made of £50 notes that makes them feel invincible. And according to research by Lloyds Bank, they tend to have an average income that's 31% higher than those with a scarcity money mindset.

Having an abundance mindset doesn't, however, guarantee financial success. You cannot out-earn a spending problem. Having an abundance mindset is like having a map of the treasure, but you still need to do the digging to find it. It won't simply appear. In fact, over three and a half million employed individuals in the UK are living in persistent 'in-work poverty', despite having jobs. Financial success isn't a given just because you earn good money.

So while it's great to be optimistic about your financial future, it's important to balance optimism with strategy. You must create a budget, set financial goals, and invest in your future as soon as you can. Individuals with an abundance mindset may feel more confident than most in their ability to earn and manage money. According to research by Aviva, individuals with an abundance mindset are more likely to take financial risks, invest in their future, and prioritise their financial goals. But without good mechanisms for due diligence and research, this can quickly go the wrong way.

Overall, having an abundance mindset can be a powerful tool for building a positive and empowered relationship with money. But financial success is not solely determined by mindset. Practical application of the Money Mechanics rules is also essential.

THE ENTITLED MONEY MINDSET

Someone with an entitled money mindset might have grown up in a household where money was used as a form of control or power. They may have learned to associate money with status and privilege and, as a result, they may feel entitled to expensive things or experiences. They might have a tendency to overspend or live beyond their means in order to maintain their perceived status or power. According to a study conducted by the Financial Conduct Authority (FCA), around one in five adults in the UK are in a position where they have debt and they cannot keep up with the minimum payments. In many cases, this is a result of overspending and living beyond their means. According to research by the Money Advice Service, 8.3 million people in the UK are currently over-indebted, which is adding to financial stress and hardship.

Studies have shown that individuals who grew up in households with high levels of income inequality compared to their peers are more likely to view money as a symbol of status and privilege. They may have perceived themselves as having a higher social status because of their wealth and this was the start of their money mindset as adults.

The entitlement could have been further reinforced if the family spent money on expensive possessions, exclusive schools and lavish holidays as, over time, money becomes a symbol of privilege and status. As adults, we become personally responsible for our finances, but if an entitled mindset persists into adulthood then this can create problems. Someone with an entitled mindset may continue to associate money with status and feel that they must spend money on expensive things to maintain their social position. If they do not have the income to back it up, overspending occurs. This is often where someone will take on debt because they are living outside of their means. They feel they deserve things regardless of whether they can actually afford them or not.

Overcoming this mindset requires a commitment to developing healthy financial habits. This can include creating a budget, setting financial goals and seeking support if needed. Additionally, seeking out resources and support can be helpful. Working with a financial advisor or joining a financial support group can provide guidance and encouragement as you work towards developing a healthier money mindset.

The entitled money mindset can be a challenging money story that can lead to financial difficulties. By acknowledging the impact of an entitled money mindset and taking steps to overcome it, you can develop a more positive and responsible relationship with money.

THE IGNORANCE MONEY MINDSET

Someone with an ignorance money mindset might have grown up in a household where money was never discussed or taught. They may have learned to avoid thinking about money or to view it as a taboo subject. As a result, they may lack basic financial literacy skills and may struggle with managing their finances as an adult.

Men have higher levels of financial literacy globally than women, with the gender pay gap ranging from three to twelve percentage points. Studies have found that younger adults (ages 18-34) have lower levels of financial literacy than older adults (ages 35-44 and 45-54), indicating a need for greater financial education and support for younger generations. This won't come as a surprise but unless you are in a private school, most students are not being taught how to engineer their money from a young age. And even in private schools, it is not a guaranteed.

The only way to fix an ignorance money mindset is to become more financially literate. If you have never been taught about money, you can't be expected to just know what to do. Investing time, effort and energy into learning will activate change for you.

If you feel like you are always up against it financially and vulnerable to unexpected expenses or financial emergencies, I can assure you there is a different way. Improving your knowledge requires a commitment to learning and implementing as you learn. This will improve how you feel about money in the long run.

THE DEBT MONEY MINDSET

If you grow up in a house where everyone skydives, then chances are, you are eventually going to jump out of a plane. It is your normal. In the same way, if you grow up in a house where debt was common, normalised or even encouraged, it is likely you will have a debt money mindset. Debt is just a standard part of life.

Living in the overdraft every month, robbing Peter to pay Paul and always borrowing to make ends meet is not how it is meant to be. Living in debt is a major buzzkill. Rationally, most of us know that, but getting out of debt feels so completely out of reach so you just carry on.

I never realised how much of a buzzkill debt was until I cleared all of mine. I simply wasn't aware of how much energy it was stealing from me. Throughout my whole adult life, I had been in some sort of debt. It was just normal to me. But actually, it isn't normal to be worried about money constantly and it can change.

According to research conducted by the Money Advice Service, over 8.3 million people in the UK have unmanageable levels of debt. In the USA, according to the Federal Reserve, things are not much better, with approximately 33% of US adults having debt that is currently in collections or has been in collections within the past year. The average US household has over $7,500 in credit card debt.

Growing up in a household where debt was commonplace can lead to a money mindset that staying in debt is just how life is. Individuals like this may see debt as a necessary part of life, or as a way to access things they otherwise couldn't afford. According to research by StepChange, over half of the UK adults that are in debt are using credit to pay for everyday expenses.

But being in debt can cause significant challenges. Not just with your financial circumstances but also with stress, anxiety, embarrassment and worry. According to research by the Financial Conduct Authority (FCA), 9% of UK adults are in severe problem debt. This can negatively impact their mental health and overall well-being. Merlyn Holkar, Senior Research Officer of Money and Mental Health found that people in problem debt are more than three times as likely to attempt suicide as those who aren't.

Overcoming a debt money mindset requires a commitment to developing healthy financial habits and making changes to reduce debt levels. This can include creating a budget, avoiding new debt and combining this with debt reduction targets, increased income or reduced expenses. We are going to be talking about these in a lot more detail in Chapter 4.

If you are someone with a debt money mindset, it might feel pretty bleak and as if you will never overcome your debt, but it will get better when you implement Money Mechanics and take proactive control of your finances. I have written a whole chapter on debt later in the book and this is going to help you.

THE GUILT MONEY MINDSET

Having a guilt money mindset is a bit like being on a roller coaster - a bumpy ride that is filled with shame or regret. Typically, people with a guilt money mindset grew up in a home where parents constantly argued about money, or there was a real lack of money.

They may have learned to feel guilty about spending money on themselves and they view money as a source of stress or conflict. As a result, they may struggle with self-care or may feel undeserving of financial success. This isn't always at a conscious level. In many cases, the feelings of being undeserving of a better financial situation sit at a subconscious level and impact everyday decisions that are being made.

In a survey conducted by the Mental Health Foundation, 24% of UK adults reported that financial issues were a source of stress. Individuals that grew up in households where money created anxiety are more likely to develop a guilt money mindset around having money, spending money or being successful financially, and this will often lead to financial self-sabotage.

People with a guilt money mindset tend to feel guilty when spending money on themselves or things that bring them happiness personally. They often feel guilty spending money on things they need like food, clothing and transportation and often opt for the cheapest possible options. Remember earlier, when we spoke about Vimes Boots theory? Someone with a guilt mindset would never buy the most expensive boots, they would always opt for the cheapest, even though the more expensive boots would actually have a more positive impact on their life.

This mindset can cause financial difficulties, such as underspending, a lack of investment in oneself and feeling stuck in a financial rut. It can also contribute to mental health issues, such as depression and anxiety, as negative thoughts and beliefs around money can lead to feelings of being trapped.

Developing healthy financial habits and prioritising self-care can help you break free from the guilt trip and improve your financial well-being and mental health. It's like planting a garden - it takes time and effort, but the results are worth it.

If you have this mindset, don't let it hold you back from living your best financial life. By taking proactive steps to change your mindset and habits, you can leave the heavy backpack behind and start walking towards a brighter financial future.

THE SUCCESS MONEY MINDSET

Are you someone that uses money to measure your worth?

Have you learned to associate how much money you have with how successful you are?

If so, you probably grew up in a home where financial success was highly valued. You have a success money mindset. As a result, you may prioritise your career or financial goals above other areas of your life, or you may feel like you are not living up to your potential if you are not financially successful right now.

Studies have shown that individuals who grew up in households where financial success was highly valued are more likely to develop a success mindset around money. In a survey conducted by the Office for National Statistics, 45% of UK adults believe that income is vital for their overall well-being.

Individuals with this mindset tend to prioritise their career or financial goals above other areas of their life. For example, they may work long hours or pursue high-paying jobs, even if it means sacrificing time with family and friends. They may do whatever it takes in their pursuit of financial success but often, their own health or mental well-being takes a back seat. They may also have a constant nagging inner narrative telling them that they are not enough simply because they don't have abundant financial success.

The success money mindset can cause stress and anxiety, as individuals may feel like they have to keep increasing their financial position in order to keep the feeling of success. Money can become quite empty with a success money mindset because it doesn't matter how much you earn, it will never be enough. It can also lead to burnout or a lack of work-life balance, as individuals may put work or financial success above their health and well-being. Not in all cases, but in many.

Striking a balance requires actions to explore the source of these beliefs and challenging them. This can include redefining what success means and finding fulfilment in other areas of life beyond just money. For example, you may start prioritising your relationships or hobbies over your career or financial goals, or at least bringing them to the same priority level. You could also seek out career opportunities that align with your values, even if the role pays less. This is only possible if you are proactively trying to make a change.

Practising self-care, setting boundaries, and finding ways to increase overall well-being can also be helpful in building a positive and balanced relationship with money. Realising that money isn't the only thing that will contribute to your happiness is a really important thing to know in life. No amount of money can bring back your mental or physical health if it goes too far in the wrong way!

THE GENEROSITY MONEY MINDSET

Someone with a generosity money mindset might have grown up in a household where giving was highly valued. They may have learned to associate money with generosity and to view giving as a way to make a positive impact in the world. As a result, they may prioritise giving their money away instead of setting boundaries around their finances.

Studies have shown that individuals who grew up in households where giving was highly valued are more likely to develop a generosity mindset around money. A survey by the Charities Aid Foundation found that 61% of UK adults donated to charity in the last year, which is fantastic. Giving more is one of the secret life hacks that so many people overlook.

That being said, individuals with a generosity mindset may prioritise giving to others over accumulating personal wealth. They may feel a sense of fulfilment from, or duty to, helping others financially, even if it means sacrificing some of their own financial resources. In extreme cases, they may also struggle with setting boundaries around their finances, as they may be more willing to help others in need than themselves. Their self-worth is formed by how much they give, however, they often miss the point that the more you have, the more you can give.

Money amplifies what is already there. If you are an arsehole, more money will make you a bigger arsehole. If you are generous, having money will facilitate you being able to be more generous.

The generosity mindset can lead to positive outcomes, such as a sense of purpose and fulfilment from making a positive impact. However, it can also lead to financial strain or lack of financial security if individuals give more than they can afford out of a misplaced sense of duty.

Building a healthy generosity mindset instead of one that works against your future wealth requires finding a balance between giving back and taking care of oneself financially. This can include setting clear boundaries around finances, such as allocating a set amount of money for charitable donations each month or year. It can also involve seeking out opportunities to give back in non-financial ways, such as volunteering time or skills while you build up your financial independence and security.

THE CONTROL MONEY MINDSET

For some people, money has been weaponised against them from a young age and used as a form of control or manipulation. If someone grows up in a home where money is used as a way of exerting control, or to manipulate others to do as they are told, then it is highly possible they will develop a control money mindset. If you have this, you would typically view financial independence as a way to assert your autonomy, which leads to prioritising financial control. As a result, you may struggle with trusting others with your finances or may have a tendency to micromanage your money and other people's money.

A control money mindset can often lead to challenges in partnerships in business, friendships and romantic relationships. Relinquishing control will lead to stress and anxiety around money, especially if money seems to be reducing rather than increasing. An impending feeling of being on the edge and losing control is not a healthy place to be.

The control money mindset can lead to positive outcomes, such as financial independence and a sense of security if managed well. However, it can also lead to negative outcomes, such as strained relationships or an inability to delegate or share financial responsibilities.

Building a healthy mindset requires finding a balance between financial independence and trusting others with financial responsibilities. This can include sharing financial responsibilities with a trusted partner or financial advisor.

The control money mindset is complex. By acknowledging the impact of a control mindset and taking steps to build a healthy relationship with money, individuals can overcome the negative impact of it. When that happens, they will experience greater financial security, positive relationships and are more likely to retain their wealth once they have built it.

THE RISK-AVERSE MONEY MINDSET

 "I prefer to keep my money in the bank where I can see it!"

This is a typical narrative for someone with a risk-averse money mindset. Someone with this mindset might have grown up in a home where financial stability was highly valued and/or highly coveted. They may have learned to associate money with security and to view financial risk as a threat to that stability. As a result, people with a risk-averse mindset avoid taking financial risks or may feel uncomfortable with investments or entrepreneurship.

In a survey by BlackRock, it was found that 70% of UK adults with low investment knowledge avoided investing in the stock market. The stock market is seen as "risky" but often that opinion is formed from stories and a lack of financial literacy. People with a risk-averse money mindset will leave their money in the bank, without realising that due to inflation, the buying power of that money is eroded every single day. We will talk about this in more detail later in the book.

Research has shown that individuals with a risk-averse mindset may miss out on opportunities for financial growth or wealth accumulation because they cannot balance the risk against the opportunity for growth. This is particularly relevant for those who are exploring investment for the first time.

Developing a healthy risk mindset requires finding a balance between financial stability and calculated and educated risk-taking. It can involve seeking out financial education or advice to understand the risks and benefits of different investment opportunities.

Setting financial goals is also an important step in developing a healthy risk mindset. By identifying specific financial goals, such as saving for retirement or buying a house, individuals can better assess the risks and benefits of different investment opportunities. They can then make more informed decisions about where to invest their money in order to achieve these goals. This proactive approach to improving a risk-averse mindset will allow you to strike a balance between financial stability and calculated risk taking. Individuals can develop a healthy risk profile that enables them to achieve their financial goals, whilst maintaining financial security.

Understanding your own personal money mindset is such an important step in developing a healthy relationship with money. Your money story, or the experiences and beliefs you have around money, shapes how you think, feel and behave when it comes to your finances. Your money mindset will ultimately control the way you react and handle debt, investing, earnings and spending. By examining your money mindset, you can identify any limiting beliefs or negative patterns that may be holding you back from achieving financial independence, stability and abundance.

To start understanding your own money mindset, I would encourage you to take a break from reading and reflect on your past experiences with money.

Consider the following questions:

1. How did your family talk about money when you were growing up?
2. What messages did you receive about money from your parents or caregivers?
3. What were your first experiences with earning and managing money?
4. How would you feel if you lost money through investments?
5. How would you feel if you made a profit from investments?

Another helpful activity is to examine your current financial habits and beliefs.

Consider how you feel about spending, saving and investing.

1. Do you feel anxious or guilty when you spend money on yourself?
2. Do you avoid taking financial risks or investing in your future?
3. Do you spend money on other people before yourself?
4. Do you protect your money at all costs?
5. Are you comfortable with the idea of losing money through investing or business?

You can download this worksheet at

www.sarahpoynton.com/moneymechanicsresources

Which money mindset are you?

You actually could be more than one!

By identifying your current financial mindset, you can begin to make conscious choices that align with the financial future that is important to you.

Your money mindset is not set in stone. You have the power to shift your mindset and develop a healthier relationship with money, risk, debt and investing. By identifying and challenging any limiting beliefs or negative patterns, you can create a more positive and abundant inner narrative.

CHAPTER 4
DECODING DEBT: STRATEGIES FOR FINANCIAL RECOVERY

D ebt is literally everywhere you turn in life right now. It is so incredibly present in everyday life but it is still one of the most misunderstood aspects of money. It is out of control for some of you, feared by many of you and avoided at all costs by others. Debt is a fundamental part of modern life. Before I move on to discuss the good and bad bits of debt, let's, first of all, get crystal clear on what it actually is.

Debt is, at its most basic level, money that is borrowed and repaid with interest over time. There are so many different forms of debt - consumer debt, mortgages, student loans, business debt, government debt, sovereign debt, liens, loans, revolving, secured, unsecured, corporate bonds... The list is long.

Debt has a terrible reputation in low-income and middle-class households, but in wealthy households, the topic of debt has a completely different reputation.

To low-income households, debt brings about bad vibes because it is generally associated with financial stress and anxiety because we don't have enough money. Extreme debt, when managed badly, results in penalties, fees or even bankruptcy. Debt to lower-income people creates a sense of uncertainty or lack of control over their finances. This reputation has been exacerbated by predatory lenders who have taken advantage of people in financial distress, leading them down the path of a never-ending cycle of debt and financial hardship.

Not all debt is created equal though.

Where a high-interest credit card can quickly spiral out of control if not managed well, a student loan is a much lower risk. Because the repayment terms are directly linked to your income, a student loan is unlikely to ever leave you in a vulnerable or exposed position. The right type of debt can actually be a very useful tool for building wealth when managed correctly. If used strategically, debt can create huge opportunities.

To give you a bit of historical context, debt has been around for as long as people have been trading goods and services. The earliest records go back to ancient civilisations such as Babylon and Mesopotamia, where temples acted as financial centres. They would offer loans to farmers, mostly.

Later, wealthy merchants and bankers started to lend money to monarchs and other nobility, which paved the way for modern banking practices. One of the most famous examples of this is when J.P. Morgan and other wealthy individuals purchased $30,000,000 in City Bonds to bail out New York City in 1907 because it didn't have enough money to pay its staff and contractors. In fear of the city collapsing and never recovering, it fell to wealthy individuals to loan money to the government, in the form of bonds, to make sure the already challenged financial markets didn't fall apart. This practice still continues today.

During the 20th century, debt became central to the global economy. There was a huge rise in consumer credit. New debt instruments such as mortgages, car loans and credit cards became commonplace. Now, debt is used for everything from business start-ups to paying for Christmas, multi-billion-dollar mergers and everything in between. This increased use of debt is where our "understanding" - or lack of it - comes from.

You will have seen the media sensationalising debt and its impact on global financial crises. You will probably have heard about Greece collapsing financially after it defaulted on a debt of 1.6 billion Euros. You will have heard about the most recent global financial crisis in 2008, which was caused, in part, by an unsustainable build-up of debt in the housing market. People, businesses and governments borrowed more than they could ever realistically repay.

All of that said, in the modern world, debt plays a huge part in driving economic growth because the wealthy, industries and governments know how to use debt to drive growth. The trouble is, they just don't share this tactic openly with us. Lower-income households typically do not leverage debt to make money, they rely on debt to finance major purchases of liabilities - things like cars and homes (like we talked about in Chapter 1). Yes, this debt helps to spread the cost of your liabilities but the debt is not helping you to become more financially independent, usually the opposite, in fact. It is keeping you stuck in an endless cycle of debt.

As we move through this chapter, I want you to understand that debt is an incredible tool for achieving financial independence but you have to know how to use it responsibly. Taking on more debt than you can handle, making late payments or defaulting will not only keep you broke, it will destroy your credit score and could create long-term financial hardship.

Debt is more than just a financial concept, it also has a very powerful psychological impact on you and your behaviour. For some, debt is a motivator, a driver that makes them hungry. For others, debt is a source of pressure, hopelessness and despair. The psychology of debt is fundamentally determined by you having a handle on the difference between good and bad debt. As I said before, not all debt is created equal.

I know that I was never taught about debt in school or growing up. I have only ever really been surrounded by people who saw debt as a burden, a thing to complain about, a negative thing. I imagine you have a similar narrative in your life, which is why you are here.

So what is the difference between good and bad debt?

Well, good debt is any type of debt that can be used to finance an investment that can generate an increase in the value of that investment - a business loan, for example. You want to start a small business, but you don't have the start-up capital that you need to buy your first batch of stock. Taking a loan, investing it into the business, and producing sales that are worth more money than the loan will allow you to repay the loan and leave you with a profit. This is just one example of good debt.

In contrast, bad debt is debt that is used to buy things that have no potential to appreciate in value or generate an income. If for example, you used a credit card to book an all-inclusive holiday to Ibiza, your club tickets, your transfers, your flights and all of your brand new clothes for the week away, this is bad debt. This debt is never going to pay you an income or increase in value. It will only ever be a debt that you are going to have to pay off yourself by draining your personal resources.

When you understand the difference between good and bad debt, you have the same power that the wealthy do. When you understand the difference between good and bad debt, you can manage it effectively. You will make the right payments, budget better and avoid taking on more debt than you can handle. Only when you know how to manage debt effectively, can you use it to build wealth over time.

Here are the top two myths about debt that the rich simply don't believe and certainly don't pay attention to as much as lower-income households do.

MYTH #1: ALL DEBT IS BAD

Some types of debt are harmful. High-interest credit cards or payday loans are definitely harmful. When I was researching this chapter, I found short-term loan solutions for individuals (not businesses) charging up to 1294% APR. APR for those of you that don't know, refers to the yearly interest that is generated/charged (by the lender) or costs/paid (by the borrower).

For a clear picture, 1294% of a £500 loan is a repayment interest amount of £6,471. No, that isn't a typo that is almost 13 times the initial amount borrowed. This type of debt is harmful, there are no two ways about it, but not all debt is going to stitch you up like this.

A buy-to-let mortgage, for example, is borrowed money but it is being put to work. It will generate rental income when you have a tenant in the property and it will also allow you to own an asset that could see an increase in value over time.

If you buy a house worth £150,000 and over 10 years the value of that house goes up to £200,000 then the loan you took out to buy it (the mortgage) has helped you create that extra £50,000 in 10 years. We will talk more about how this works in the property chapter but this type of debt is a great tool for building your wealth.

MYTH #2: DEBT ALWAYS LEADS TO FINANCIAL RUIN

Excessive debt is harmful, but responsible use (leverage) of other people's money can actually help build your credit and increase wealth.

Firstly, let's talk about how it can build your credit score.

By making regular payments, on time and in full, your financial footprint will be seen in a more positive light. Let's say you take out a £500 loan and you pay back every penny on time and in full over a twelve-month period. That is going to put you in a more positive position when it comes to being considered for any type of lending in the future.

Financial ruin comes from not paying back what you have borrowed, on time and in full. People go wrong when they miss payments by accident, or they simply don't pay. Instead of the debt working in their favour, the debt will hit on their credit file negatively.

Plus, missed and late payments lead to unnecessary fees and charges.

If that continues, financial ruin could well be the result.

But some debt, when managed well and repaid in full and on time, is actually a very positive tool in your journey to financial independence. We know this because, if you take a look at Elon Musk, he used debt to buy Twitter. He used his other assets as collateral for the debt, but he used debt for the actual acquisition. Adele is reported to have recently purchased a new home in LA using a mortgage. Now why would Adele do this when she has more than enough cash to buy it outright? The answer is the leverage of other people's money. Because keeping hold of her own cash means she can invest it elsewhere. If invested well, it has the power to make more money than the debt is costing, so she is using leverage to increase her wealth and is using invested cash to pay for a liability. Had Adele simply tied up that money, she would have drained her own resources. Slight disclaimer - Adele and I, sadly, are not friends so we haven't talked this through, but I know that most of the extremely wealthy people I know and spoke to when researching for this book told me that they do exactly the same thing. Invested cash is what pays the mortgages on their own homes so that they never drain their personal resources to own a home.

The other great thing about leverage is that you don't pay taxes on debt. Elon Musk got a huge influx of cash, tax-free, that he leveraged to acquire an asset which now (should) generate an income and appreciate over time. Adele got an influx of cash, tax-free, that she leveraged to acquire a home, which could increase in value over time, but also allowed her to retain control of her own money.

For rich people, debt doesn't result in financial ruin. Rich people leverage debt as much as they can and use it to become even more wealthy.

I often get asked about how to pay off debt. This is a topic I know a lot about and it is a very personal journey for us all. In 2015, I had roughly £60,000 worth of bad debt. It was a combination of things including loans, credit cards and overdrafts. I remember the feeling very well and whilst, right now, I don't have any bad debt, I know first-hand just how easy it is to get into bad debt and just how hard it is to get out of it once you are there.

You see, for the lenders - the banks and credit card companies - it is in their best interests to keep you in debt. That is how they make their money. They lend out money for a fee. That fee is their profit. Of course, they don't want to make it easy for you to clear that debt. Quite the opposite, in fact.

The three biggest questions I get asked about clearing debt are:

1. What debt should I pay off first?
2. What should I actually do to clear my debt?
3. Should I clear my debt before I invest or invest before I clear my debt?

So, I want to tackle these three things for you.

WHAT DEBT SHOULD I PAY OFF FIRST?

When you are in debt, it can feel very emotional and often you can't see the answers because it is all just a little (or a lot) overwhelming. To effectively tackle debt head-on, you need a plan that prioritises the debt in an order that you can then stick to. Once you have determined which one to clear first, you have to stick to it.

One way you can prioritise debt reduction is by looking at what that debt is actually costing you. I don't know about you but when I was deep in debt, I didn't really understand how to work out what it was costing me. I am going to break this down into the simplest form I can so you know exactly what it all means.

You are being charged to borrow money. That is shown by the interest rate that you are being charged, which will be shown on your statements. By focusing on the debt that is charging you the highest interest rates, you will save the most money and churn through your debt liability faster.

Imagine you have:

Credit card debt of £5,000 with an interest rate of 18% (£900 per year)

Plus

A car finance loan of £10,000 with an interest rate of 5% (£500 per year)

Plus

A personal loan of £3,000 with an interest rate of 10% (£300 per year)

Total debt is £18,000

Not all debt is equal, remember!

If you were to focus on paying off the credit card first, you would save £900 in interest charges over the year. But if you focused on the personal loan first you would save £300 in charges over the year. By making larger payments on the highest-costing debt first (whilst still meeting the minimum payments on your other debts) you accelerate your progress towards becoming debt free.

This was the method I used in 2015 to tackle my £60,000 debt. It is known as 'The Avalanche Method'. As I cleared the balance on the most expensive debt, I would cut the card up and throw it away. That meant I still had the available balance, (which can work in your favour when it comes to your credit score) but I had no way of using it on impulse. If I wanted access to the balance, I would have to call the bank, sit on hold for hours and order a new card, wait for the card to arrive and then spend. It removed the impulse spending from my life completely and it removed the risk of being on a night out and blowing a load of money on my credit card because I'd had too many Jack Daniels & Coke. Yes, this totally happened way too many times! The plastic made it too easy.

This tactic meant my credit score continued to improve and I had taken away the possibility of me buying shit I didn't need and taking myself back to square one.

There is another debt repayment method called 'The Snowball' method. This is where you take all the different debt lines that you have and you start chipping away at the ones with the lowest balances first. If you are someone that likes to feel the win quickly, then this method will be great for you. It has a powerful, positive impact on your mindset as you tackle your debt.

Imagine you have:

Credit card debt of £1,000

Plus

A Car loan of £10,000

Plus

An overdraft of £350

Plus

Another credit card of £750

The snowball method would see you tackle the £350 overdraft first, then the £750 credit card, then the £1,000 credit card and then the car loan. You will have to meet the minimum payments on them all to stay in line with your loan terms, but you overpay on the one with the smallest balance first. By focusing on the size of the debt you eliminate the number of different places you are indebted to much faster.

The sense of accomplishment that comes from being able to say "that one is cleared" will be a really positive motivator to continue on the journey of clearing the rest. The quicker wins feel great from a mindset perspective. You really feel like you are making progress.

SHOULD YOU CLEAR YOUR DEBT OR INVEST FIRST

The answer to this question is actually easier than you would think to answer. You need to adhere to the rule of seven - that is, 7%.

When deciding between investing or clearing debt, you have to work out if the debt is costing you more than 7%. If it is costing you more than 7% a year then it makes sense to get rid of it first. If it is costing you less than 7% then you could consider the possibility of investing and using the profits from the investment to clear the debt. This has some risk attached to it of course, as investing has risk. That being said, some of the lowest-risk investments available typically return more than 7% per year, so many people opt to invest and use the profits to clear their debt if their debt is costing less than 7%. If it is over 7% then generally people will opt to clear the debt first. You have to determine your own personal circumstances and, of course, carry out due diligence (which we will discuss in a later chapter), then make the decision of whether you should invest first or clear your debt first.

The first step in any of this is to first assess where you are.

Now, the next thing I am going to share with you is something that most people don't like to do, especially if you are someone that knows you are in debt but don't really know exactly how bad it is. Maybe you don't really know what it is costing you, as long as you are holding your minimum payments together and keeping your head above water, you just keep ticking along. That was me in 2015. I was terrified of looking at all the bills together, it just felt so overwhelming. So, this bit might be painful, but it is time to tear the plaster off and get clear on where you are. It is only when we know where we are that we can improve things.

This was one of the best decisions I ever made.

I need you to assess your debts. Take a break from reading and write a list of all your debts. Use the table below as a template or go to www.sarahpoynton.com/moneymechanicsresources to download the template I created for you.

Debt Owed To	Debt Amount	Interest Rate	Type Of Debt	Months Left To Pay	Good Or Bad

Total Good Debt _____

Total Bad Debt _____

Well done! You are amazing! Great work.

Now you know where you are in terms of your debt.

If you have got through that and not just shredded this book then I am really proud of you. That bit is tough! Honestly, that step is the hardest part when it comes to clearing debt.

Now you are a Money Mechanic, you can work on activating change by implementing everything else you are about to learn.

So how do you do that?

I use the B.A.A.T system for getting debt under control.

Create a **B**UDGET

AVOID new debt

AUTOMATE your money

TRACK your progress

CREATE A BUDGET

The first stage of having a budget is knowing how much is coming in. I am often surprised by how many people don't actually know this. I know, in some cases, your final monthly figure will vary from month to month. If you are employed at the moment, the reason for this is usually down to the joys of tax. However, unless you have a role like sales, where you get varied commissions every month based on performance, or you have a role that always varies hours from week to week, then your salary will be almost the same each month. You need to know that number.

If you are in a role that pays you commissions, then work with your consistent baseline figure in the same way that someone in a role without commissions can. If you are in a role that gives you five hours this week and fifteen hours next week and 3 hours the following week, then budgeting will be really difficult. I would have a think about how you could even that out with some kind of secondary income (side hustle) that could work around the varied nature of your job.

Once you know how much is coming in each month then you will want to start thinking about what you need to spend on essentials, what qualifies as an essential, and what is nice to have, based on your own personal values.

Now listen, for some people, their favourite £25 shampoo is essential because it makes them feel like themselves, hair on point, it can bring confidence and joy. For others, the thought of spending £25 on a bottle of shampoo is insane. I am not here to judge, we all have our own unique ways and they are all the right way!

I am a girl that will happily spend £36 on a Dior mascara but I would never spend £7.50 on a tub of named-brand butter or spread. One of my very best friends would happily invest £4,000 in a Prada handbag but refuses to ever pay full price for a tub of Pringles. Value-based spending is the key here and when you engineer your money through debt control and investing, you won't have to go without. You will have enough for everything you need, long into the future. But to begin with, you have to budget.

When putting your budget together you must consider your fixed expenses and your variable expenses. Variable just means it is always changing, fixed means it is the same every time. A fixed rate mortgage is a fixed expense, it is normally the same every month for the term of your agreement. Rent payments are a fixed expense. Car payments are a fixed expense. Variable expenses are things like petrol, personal care, utilities, food, and socialising. Add into your budget your fixed expenses first and then your variable expenses second.

Have you got a contingency fund? If not, you need to start building one. This is the pot of money you can rely on if things go wrong. This is your safety net for when the unexpected happens.

If your car is stolen today, do you have a contingency pot to pay your excess on your insurance, or buy a new car? If your boiler breaks today, do you have £2,100 for a new one?

Your contingency fund is how you can always be prepared for financial emergencies. If you don't have this then the only way to pay for these occurrences is either to whack it on a credit card or to go without in some other aspect of your life. Neither of these is actually going to have a positive impact on you. Having your contingency fund is going to mean you don't ever have to panic. If you don't have one yet then this will want to make its way into your budget as a top priority, before you start thinking about investing.

If you don't know how to start with a budget, I have created a budget template that will speed this up for you. If you head over to www.sarahpoynton.com/moneymechanicsresources you can download my budget tracker. It is already set up, so all you have to do is plug in your own numbers and it will calculate everything for you.

AVOID NEW DEBT

Once you have a budget set, you move onto step 2 of the B.A.A.T system and that is to AVOID new debt!

Avoiding new debt can be challenging. We have already talked about having your emergency fund. Having an emergency fund will start to take the burden away from your debt if/when unexpected things happen. In an ideal world, you want to aim to build this up to a minimum of three times your monthly fixed living costs. This might take three months for some of you, and it might take three years for others but the existence of this emergency fund will help you to avoid new debt when things go wrong. Even if you are putting just a few pounds a month into a pot for this, the sooner you start, the sooner you will be at your emergency fund target.

Learning to live below your means is something that will help you to avoid new debt. I think the world has got it twisted. Too many people live above their means to try and look on the surface like they are wealthy. The house, the car, the holidays, the 'show'. Remember, I said the point of all this is to actually be wealthy and not just to look rich on the surface level of your life.

This is what I see lots of people doing. They get a £1,000 a year pay rise, so they start to spend more. They move jobs to a brand new company and get an amazing increase of £10,000 a year, but they start living like Rockefeller, spending £10,000 a year more, forgetting about tax and deductions and good money management. As people earn more, they are eligible for bigger mortgages, bigger credit cards and bigger car loans, and all of a sudden not only are they not seeing that extra £10,000 a year in their pocket. They are spending way more than that a year and so are actually worse off than they were earning less. You can't out-earn a spending problem!

Living below your means is the most underrated hack when it comes to getting your money under control. Avoid the temptation to spend more than you have. Focus on living below your income level and contributing to your future financial position instead of living for instant gratification. You can't have both (to begin with) but you can have both eventually! Use the budget tracker on my website to really get crystal clear on the details surrounding your income and spending.

Learn to negotiate on everything. If your broadband is going up, call them and secure a better deal or change suppliers; if your contents insurance is renewed, call them and get a better deal. I know this is extra life admin, but if you can save £10 a month on your broadband, £10 a month on your house insurance and £10 a month on your car insurance that is £30 a month you could be putting straight into your investment pot. £30 a month for 12 months, compounded at 10% per year over 15 years, gives you £12,567.73. Just because you made the effort to negotiate a little bit!

I will talk about how you actually compound your money over time in a later chapter. Now you are a Money Mechanic, that old narrative of "it is only £10 a month, what difference will it make" can switch to "That money is better in my bank than theirs so I can invest it". This attitude to small, seemingly insignificant amounts will tangibly change your wealth over time. And in this case, that money is created by simply asking for a better deal on things you are already paying for. Seems simple, doesn't it?

Because it is. It is these small steps towards change that matter the most to your success as a Money Mechanic.

AUTOMATE YOUR MONEY

Now let's talk about automating your money. You might have heard about the envelope system or money pots. If you are over on TikTok, you will know there are literally hundreds of channels that talk about the envelope system for managing your money, but for me, cash laying around my house in envelopes just doesn't work. It is too hands-on and relies really heavily on my being disciplined, which I am not naturally very good at. You may be surprised to hear but I have to actually work really hard at this stuff and make conscious choices. Instead of envelopes, I use online banking to automate my money in every way I possibly can.

There are lots of ways you can automate your money.

The first is direct debits/standing orders. When you have a fixed expense that is always going to be the same, these are helpful. If you know your rent is due on the 1st of the month, every month, then you might as well set that up as an automatic payment. It gives you one less thing to think about. Then think about what we have talked about in relation to your credit cards. Set up the amount you have budgeted towards your debt to be paid to your credit card on the same day every month. Remember a Money Mechanic doesn't just pay the minimum payment. You pay what you have budgeted above your minimum payment to reduce the cost of the debt and increase the speed you will be paying it off. Bill payments like this will always work better when you set them up to be paid automatically. If you do this manually then you are relying on your own discipline. Can you 100% trust that you won't forget, or simply spend it on other things?

Now, to take this a layer deeper, let's talk about automating your money with pots. This is one of my favourite things to talk about because I actually think my state of financial independence came from introducing pots into my life. Without them, I don't think it would have mattered how much money I earned, I would have spent it all. As I said above, it doesn't matter how much money you make if you don't understand the mechanics of putting it to work, so what I am about to tell you is going to change the game for you!

In 2017, I read a book called Profit First, by Mike Michalowicz. I read it with my business finances in mind. I wanted to learn how to run the finances in my business as well as I could because my first business was such a disaster financially. I wanted to bring in best practices that would really make a difference in making sure my money management was exceptional.

After reading this book, I engineered the money in my business like this:

Of every pound that comes into the business this happens:

20% is moved to an account that is labelled Corporation Tax

20% is moved to an account that is labelled Value Added Tax

20% is moved to an account that is labelled Profit

And the 40% that is left, I operate the business from.

I never touch my Corporation Tax bill pot and I never touch my VAT bill pot because really, that is not my money. It is the tax man's money. However, because I run a system of 20% of turnover and not 20% of profit, both of those pots always have more in them than I will ever owe to the tax man. This means I will never have an unexpected tax bill that I can't afford to pay. I automate the money in the business daily. It doesn't matter if £1 comes in or £15,000 I will do that same task and move the money in the right proportions to the right pots.

After I read this book and implemented it in my work life, I realised that I could take control of my personal money in the same way. I bank with Monzo (there is a joining link at the end of this chapter) and Chase. In my Monzo and Chase accounts, I have set up pots and I use those pots to automate my money.

This is how I do it:

I have pots set up as follows:

1. My Fuck about fund (FAF) - I have this in my Chase account. This is money that is for me to do what I want. Chase has a feature that will "round up" spending. That means that when I spend £3.65 on something on my card, Chase automatically rounds up to the next full £1 and moves the difference from my main account to my FAF. In this case, it would be 35p added. Then Chase pays me 5% interest on all the money in that account. I also have a £10 a week drip set up to go into this pot if there is enough in my main account. If there isn't, nothing gets moved. Monzo also has the roundup feature, but at the time of writing this they don't pay 5% on the account so for me, Chase trumps Monzo because it is creating passive income for me by mopping up the pennies from the pounds I am already spending. It soon adds up as well. In 2022, I used my FAF to pay for flights abroad.

2. My Give to charity fund - Every year I donate what is in this pot to a charity of my choice. I move £5 a week into this pot and I don't touch it unless it is to donate it to charity or sponsor someone in something they are doing like running a marathon or a skydive for example. Now you might not have £5 a week, you might only have 50p a month, but whatever you have it is important to make sure you have a pot that is for you to give away, donate or use to enrich someone else. This might seem counterintuitive to give your money away but remember, money flows like energy so if you contribute to others, you are more likely to see a positive enrichment in your world in return. I use my Monzo account for this.

3. Joint Bills money - This is our house bills pot. Our mortgage, our utilities, my husband and my combined non-negotiable expenses. For us, it is £1,000 a month each that goes into this pot. If you are someone that lives alone, this layer of your money is often the most difficult to handle, because you don't have the privilege of splitting the bill. This is why it is even more important for you to be engineering your money and putting it to work so that you are financially independent without the need to split the bill with someone else. I use Monzo for this.

4. Insurances - this is my car insurance, house insurance, our pet insurance for our three fluffballs, and my life insurance. Even if you pay annually, it is worth putting something away monthly so that you don't have to find it when the renewal date comes around. My husband taught me this when we met. He always paid in advance for his insurance and that was so alien to me as I had always just paid monthly, but it will save you quite a bit of money across all your policies. You will have to work really hard for a year paying it twice but in year two, you will be saving substantial amounts that can be invested instead. I move the exact amount of these bills to that pot on payday and when the automated payments come out, they come out of that pot instead of out of my main account, that way I know I will never miss a payment and I will always be insured.

5. Petrol - I move £25 a month into this account. My husband and I share a car so I don't actually spend much on petrol myself. He tends to fill the car up when he sees the lowest prices. Sharing a car was a decision we made in 2022 because having one set of car expenses every year allowed us to take around £4,000 a year and invest it instead of spending it. This is around £333 a month, which compounded over five years at 10% per year is a pot worth £26,334.43, instead of us having £20,000 outgoing in the same time frame. A swing of £46,334.43 over five years just by being a bit more organised with the way we use our vehicle. And I get it, I used to say there is no way we could operate with one car. It began for us in September 2022, when my Audi went back to the leasing company. We were going travelling for the rest of the year around Europe in our motorhome so we decided not to replace my car until after the New Year. But then the New Year came around, we were coping fine without a second car and so decided to just stick with one. It might not be forever but it is already making a big difference to our investment pots.

You will need to choose the amount that is right for you in your budget and do your best to stick to it!

1. Personal Tax - sadly this is unavoidable. Make sure you have the best tax advice you can get and be as tax efficient as you possibly can be. If you are paid on P.A.Y.E, your personal tax contributions are taken at the source by your employer, so you won't need to worry about this. If, like me, you are self-employed, you will need to make sure you are building up your tax pot every month to pay the bill at the end of the year. Ask your accountant what your % will be, based on your income level, and put that money aside every month. Trust me, you don't want the tax man chasing you because you haven't put enough aside to pay the bill. Better to work ahead and automate this every month.

2. Car Finance - We pay a finance fee for our car. £346.98 a month and that payment comes straight out of my current account on payday. It is automatically moved to the Car Finance pot. It sits in the pot until the date it has to be paid to our provider. When it is paid it comes automatically out of the car finance pot. I use Monzo for this as well.

3. Rainy Day Savings - This is my emergency fund as we have already talked about, which sits at between three and six months of living expenses for me. If I have used it for something that is classified as an emergency then I top it up, if not, I just leave it there. It earns 3% per annum in Monzo. This is not great because, with inflation, this is eroding daily, however, it does help me sleep at night knowing it is there and it helps me know I am independent and doing things I choose to do and not making decisions because I can't afford to change my mind. In this account, the money is not locked in but it does take three days to transfer out, so the temptation of an impulse buy is removed completely. I use Monzo for this but there may well be other accounts that you could use for this. I know at the time of writing, Barclays was offering a Rainy Day Saver that paid 5% interest per annum. It is worth exploring options for this. Don't leave your emergency pot in an account that is not generating interest. Even if it is just a small bit, it all makes a difference.

4. Investing - This is the pot that I invest from and I will talk to you more about this in the investing chapter. For now though, know that whatever you have allowed for investing in your budget, even if it is £1 a week to start with, MUST be separated from your other money in the same automated way all your other commitments are. When investing is new to you, it is really easy to move from month to month and forget to do it. By automating this, you will be able to really maximise your investments - firstly, because you will actually do it, and secondly, because you can take advantage of dollar cost averaging, which might not make any sense yet but it will by the end of the book.

5. Saving for.... - There are things that come up that you will want to splash out on or that you need to save up for in advance to be able to afford them. Maybe Christmas, maybe a holiday, a new coat, a watch, an engagement ring, a festival ticket, or a course to improve your skills in your chosen profession. Whatever you are saving up for, you need a pot for it - or multiple pots if you have multiple things on the horizon. Contribute to it little and often in line with your budget and you will have the thing sooner than you think. This will mean you don't drain your resources in a big hit and you won't have to take on bad debt to have the things you want.

You will set your pots up differently based on your own budget but the principle of what I have shared is what you must implement in order to really make a difference to your financial independence.

Take a break from reading and go and set up your pots! If your bank doesn't do pots then head to the link at the bottom of this page to set up Monzo. They do a speedy account switch which was seamless when I did it and that link will also gift you with £5. At the time of writing this, Monzo is only available if you have a UK address. Chase has facilities in other parts of the world. If you are in a country that doesn't have either it is likely you will have a bank that can facilitate the pots system.

Here is a link to join Monzo if you don't already bank with them https://join.monzo.com/c/hrxb3j4 If you use that link we both get £5 added to our account for free!

Happy days!

TRACKING YOUR PROGRESS

Once it is set up and things are ticking along, you must track your progress. Check in on your budget regularly and update it monthly.

Peter Drucker famously said, "What gets measured gets improved". You are a Money Mechanic now. Gone are the days of not checking our accounts, just hoping the plastic will ping ok when you swipe it at the shop. From today onwards, you take control of your money. It is the only way to clear your debt and give yourself a foundation from which to invest and grow your wealth into the future.

Remember, if you read this book and change nothing then nothing is going to change.

I personally do this on the last day of every month - a process I call 'month end'. It started as a process in my business but it has become a monthly activity in my personal finances as well. I check in with my budget and I update my assets and liabilities tracker so that I know exactly where I am with my money and my net worth all the time.

I know it feels overwhelming to track and check in with your money as regularly as this but if you implement these steps, things will start to change for you. You will be running your money, instead of your money running you.

CHAPTER 5
BRICK BY BRICK: CREATING WEALTH THROUGH PROPERTY INVESTMENT

P roperty investment, real estate; wherever you are in the world it may be called a different name but the fundamentals are the same. At its core, property investment is where you control bricks and mortar assets with the intention of generating income and/or capital growth. Real estate assets are often favoured because the business model has a very tangible existence. You can walk into a property, you can see it, touch it and feel it. You can visit it and no one can run off with it, it can't be packed up and stolen. It is tangible and many people feel like it is less risky because of this.

However, as with any mechanism used to create wealth, there are risks associated with property investment. In this chapter, you are going to explore the basics of investing in property including the pros and cons, so that you have a better understanding and an increased awareness of how you can invest in property sooner than you probably thought possible.

This is a long chapter, I want to tell you that right now. I have broken it into two sections, the first is about making money by buying and renting property, the second is all about making money from property without ever buying or renting anything. Both are amazing, but grab a cuppa before you dive into this chapter of the book.

Before I get into how property works let me tell you a little about the journey I have been on with property myself.

In 2015, when I was around £60,000 in debt and had a failing business and no bloody clue how I was going to get myself out of that mess, it was the property world that presented itself to me. Now, I don't know if that was by design or if that was just clever advertising done by the people whose ads I clicked on, but I began to learn about some of the property investment business models that exist outside of the traditional buy-to-let routes. What I discovered was eye-opening, to say the least.

I don't know about you, but until I really started to dig into what was possible in property, I had only really ever been exposed to property via programmes such as Property Ladder, Million Dollar Listing, Love It or List It, Homes Under The Hammer, Selling Sunset and Location Location Location, most of which showed people buying property to add some value to it and sell it at a later date for a profit. I had no idea that there were actually lots of different avenues to making money in property. I assumed that to get started in property, I needed to actually have money, which I definitely did not have. I could barely afford the house I was living in, let alone afford to start adding houses to my portfolio.

It wasn't until 2015 that I started to better understand that actually, anyone can start creating wealth through property, even if they don't have savings themselves yet. You really can start generating income from property almost immediately. This chapter is going to help you understand all of the options available to you, regardless of where you are right now in terms of savings.

Property brings many benefits to the table:

1. There is potential for capital appreciation. This is where the thing you own goes up in value over time - its capital value appreciates. If you sell it when the value is higher than what you paid for it then you keep the profit (after taxes of course). There are also ways you can borrow against the value of the property which means, in many cases, you don't need to sell the property to realise the increase in value. This way, you can use the capital appreciation as a tool to buy another property. You can recycle your money over and over again if you buy right. We will talk in detail about leverage in Chapter 13.

2. Most real estate investments will generate income. It isn't usually completely passive because, even if you have a management team in place, that team needs to be managed. Usually, if you own or control a building and you rent it out to people to live there, work there or operate a business from there, they will pay you rent. That rent becomes an income.

3. Property is typically a hedge against inflation. If you look at the data of historic housing prices compared to inflation, you will see that in times of increased inflation, rents and property values tend to increase as well. So while the buying power of your money in your savings account is going down when inflation increases, the value of your property assets is usually going up. Using property investing to balance out these scales is the Money Mechanics way.

4. You have overall control of how your properties are managed. This is different to when you own a share in a company. If you own a share in Apple, Google or Amazon then, in reality, you have no real input into the performance of the company. When you own and rent out residential, commercial or agricultural, in fact, any property, you have the power and the option to be in total control of how that portfolio is managed. You can outsource the work but you choose who you outsource to. You can hire people but you would be in control of how those people are making decisions around your portfolio, so you have total control, which is a really attractive proposition for many people.

5. To buy property you can leverage other people's money. I have written a whole chapter on leverage later in the book. Leverage is such an important aspect of being a Money Mechanic. Where property is concerned, you would use other people's money to acquire the assets and add value to the assets. Sometimes, this is money from the bank. This is institutional money. In other cases, you may work with high-net-worth private investors who have savings or funds from other business activities that they want to put to work. Borrowed funds can be secured against the property as collateral, the investor makes a profit and you make money - money that you wouldn't have been able to make had you not leveraged other people's money.

However, getting involved in the property world shouldn't be seen as a get-rich-quick business. It is an industry that comes with its own set of risks.

1. It is not easy to liquidate your money. This means you can't get to it quickly. In an emergency, you are unlikely to be able to rely on using any funds you have in the property world as your solution. If you did need the cash fast, it is likely you would have to sell at a huge discount in order to access it. Selling a house in the UK takes an average of sixteen weeks currently. In the USA, the average is around thirteen weeks. In parts of Europe, it can take up to twenty weeks at the time of writing this. For most people, if your money is in bricks-and-mortar assets, you can only get the money out by selling that asset to someone else or refinancing (borrowing) money secured against the asset. If you need money fast, this would create a problem.

2. Unexpected expenses. We talked in the debt chapter about how important it is to keep on top of your expenses. Property is quite unpredictable in this sense. Unexpected repairs and maintenance will eat into your profits. Tenants not paying their rent will leave you paying for mortgages out of your own resources. Tax rules change often and interest rates are ever-changing. In the last three months alone, I have had interest rate increases, a tenant that hasn't paid their rent for three months, eviction costs, redecoration costs of a three-bedroom house, a full end-of-tenancy clean, a broken window, a toilet flush that has been snapped, a blocked drain, a kitchen cooking hob needing replacing, two replacement doors, the need for a brand new boiler and a broken dishwasher. That is across my portfolio, not all in one property, but it was all unexpected. Anything unexpected impacts your ability to remain a savvy Money Mechanic. You must factor in this risk, and a good Money Mechanic will always set aside a buffer each month for unexpected costs like this. In the same way, we have an emergency fund in our real life, we have an emergency fund in our property life too.

3. Tenant issues. Every type of tenant is different but in the UK in 2022, the average time it took to evict a difficult or non-paying residential tenant was 44.5 weeks. That, combined with the £355 possession application fee, the warrant of eviction fee of £130, the high court transfer fee of £35, county court bailiff fees of £350, or high court bailiff fees of £1,200 to evict one difficult or non-paying tenant, is a huge risk. On top of that, if a tenant isn't paying, you will need to fund their eviction and the mortgage on the property yourself, if there is one. In other parts of the world, these amounts differ and the rules are different everywhere but tenant issues exist everywhere and they can be unpredictable.

4. Interest rates are unstable. At the time of writing this, we are seeing interest rates move upwards globally from a long period of the lowest rates we have seen since the financial crisis of 2008. This means that it is likely that interest rates will continue to be volatile or actually continue to rise for the foreseeable future. This becomes a problem for you, as a landlord, if the mortgage payments to the bank each month become higher than the rent you could charge on a property. You would be losing money by providing a home to someone. Since 2008, many people have geared extremely highly and have made their portfolios work at unsustainably low interest rates. Those people will be really stuck at the point when their mortgage rates are up for renewal. Interest rate rises have the potential to force a loss unless a landlord pushes up rents.

5. Property taxes are also different everywhere but there will also be tax to contend with. There is capital gains tax that you pay when you sell, corporation tax if you make a profit (if you own property in a business), income tax if you take an income from your portfolio, stamp duty land tax that you pay when you buy and in the UK, you cannot offset the cost of borrowing (the interest rate) against your tax bill as an operational expense. People outside of property won't know this, but it is the only industry in the UK where the genuine operational costs of running the business cannot be offset against tax. In simple terms, this means that as a UK landlord, you will be made to pay tax on money you have never actually received, so it is really important to assess your numbers accurately in order to be sure you are not overexposed to these risks.

Many of the risks I have mentioned have nuances in different parts of the world and certainly, the tax issues are not global. There are risks associated with real estate in every market though.

There is a record number of residential landlords selling up and leaving the market in all major countries because the risks and rates are beginning to outweigh the benefits for many. My thoughts on this are that property is moving away from being a cash flow business and becoming more of an asset management business. Asset management is the practice of increasing wealth over time by acquiring, maintaining and trading investments over long periods of time - an incredible opportunity for us all when you understand how.

Now I have terrified you about all the things that could go wrong, let's talk a little bit about how you could get started in the property world, if you think you have the stomach for it!

Before starting down the property investing avenue you really need to define your goals and objectives. You need an investment strategy that takes into consideration:

- Your personal circumstances
- Your risk tolerance
- Your investment timeline
- The outcome you are looking to achieve from your investments
- The outcome you are looking to achieve for your life
- How much money you have got access to, to begin with

There are some important questions to ask and answer before making any big investment decisions.

1. Are you looking for passive income or hands-on income?
2. How much capital do you have to invest right now?
3. How much risk are you comfortable taking?
4. Do you want to be a landlord and have tenants?
5. How long do you plan to hold your portfolio?
6. Do you want to have a social impact or are you just in it for cash?
7. How diversified do you want to be?

As you start to answer some of these questions, you will begin to get a picture of what outcome you are looking for from property, which in turn means you can invest in a way that matches what you want to achieve.

Now, property might not be for you... yet, but I would recommend that you continue reading this chapter because some of the business models I am going to share with you blew my mind when I first learned them - so much so that I was able to start a property business that turned over just under £100,000 in its first twelve months, from a starting state of £60,000 debt, a terrible credit score and no bloody clue what I was doing. If I can do it then you totally can as well.

THE DIFFERENT PROPERTY BUSINESS MODELS EXPLAINED

Buy-to-Let - This is the most commonly understood property business model. You buy a property and you rent it out to a tenant. Simple. The numbers look a little bit like this:

Description	Amount
Purchase Price	£200,000

Mortgage (75% LTV)	-£150,000

Equity	£50,000
Monthly Rental Income	£1,500

Annual Rental Income	£18,000
Monthly Mortgage Payments	-£750
Monthly Management Costs	-£150
Monthly Maintenance Costs	-£75
Monthly Insurance	-£50

Monthly Miscellaneous Costs	-£50
Monthly Net Income	£525

Annual Net Income	£6,300
Gross Yield	9.00%
Net Yield	3.15%
ROI	12.60%

In the above example profits are listed before tax. This is a sample summary to highlight the basics. The above formula has not allowed for Stamp Duty Land Tax or legal costs to acquire as these numbers vary vastly throughout the UK and depend on annual changes by HMRC.

Useful Calculations To Be Aware Of:

The gross yield is calculated by dividing the annual rental income by the purchase price, multiplied by 100%. In this case, it is (£18,000 / £200,000) x 100% = 9.00%.

The net yield is calculated by dividing the annual net income by the purchase price, multiplied by 100%. In this case, it is (£6,300 / £200,000) x 100% = 3.15%.

The ROI (Return on Investment) is calculated by dividing the annual net income by the total investment, multiplied by 100%. In this case, it is (£6,300 / £50,000) x 100% = 12.60%.

There will be different lines in the expenses and different amounts associated in different parts of the world but you will get the idea of how the numbers tend to work on a buy-to-let property investment from the sample above.

In the example above, the total monthly expenses for the buy-to-let are £1,075, including the mortgage, management, insurance and maintenance costs. The total income is £1,500 per month, resulting in a profit per month of £525 before taxes. These are sample numbers and every property is different. Some properties make more than this every month and others make less. Some even produce a negative figure every month, based on the unpredictability of expenses and interest rates. We have a mortgage-free, three-bedroom house that rents out at £500 a month, but last month the drains were blocked and a drainage pipe needed to be replaced. The invoice for investigation, parts and labour was £743. Some months it just happens like that.

ROI and Yield are both numbers that we use to measure the performance and profitability of an investment. Knowing these figures takes the emotion out of things and allows you to compare investments in a very logical and rational way. They both represent a very different thing though.

Return On Investment (ROI) looks at the amount invested (how much you physically handed over) and how well that total amount is generating a return for you. It is calculated by dividing the gain from the investment by the total amount invested and giving the result as a percentage. ROI gives insight into the overall profitability of an investment.

If you buy a property for £100,000 and sell it for £120,000, the profit is £20,000 and the ROI is 20% (£20,000 gain / £100,000 x 100). There isn't a fixed number that makes an investment good or bad. Everyone has their own criteria for this, but the higher number, the better.

Yield is different and measures the income generated relative to the total sum incurred to acquire that asset in the first place. It is calculated by dividing the annual income generated by the total investment price, expressed as a percentage. Yield gives you an insight into the ongoing income that will come from an investment.

If you buy a property for £200,000 and it generates £18,000 in annual income through rent, the yield is 9% (£18,000 income / £200,000 x 100) In the UK, according to propertydata.co.uk, the average yield is currently 4.75%. In the USA it is 6.12% and in Canada 5.46%.

The thing about buy-to-let is that you do need to buy a property. You cannot do buy-to-let unless you physically buy a property and rent it out. That takes cash upfront. This is the most traditional option and the most well-known but it is slow because you need money to get going.

Investors are forever finding faster, more effective ways to make money and so there are a few other property business models to tell you about.

CREATIVE PROPERTY INVESTMENT BUSINESS MODELS

Rent-to-Rent: This business model is vastly different from buy-to-let. Rent-to-rent is one of the main business models I ran in my property business for the first four years - four years that completely changed my financial position and four years that taught me an awful lot about being a landlord, how to manage tenants, how to run a business and more. I don't have a rent-to-rent business anymore. It no longer suited my personal objectives and my business evolved as I discovered more and became more financially independent and abundant. Would I do it again if I was starting again? Absolutely, but it isn't right for everyone. This business model will always hold a pretty special place in my heart because it really did teach me a lot. It helped me to generate high cash flow, quickly, without needing huge amounts of money to begin with.

The way it works is that you become a tenant in a property and then you gain consent from the owner to sublet that property to someone else, or multiple people. It is a really well-known business model in the commercial world but not as well understood in the residential world. You may have heard of WeWork. This was a serviced office provider that was one of the highest-valued businesses, alongside Airbnb and Space X, in 2018. Their business model was to rent giant commercial properties, split them up into smaller offices and hot-desking facilities and then re-rent (sublet) the smaller spaces out to the customers. WeWork collapsed in 2019 due to a 'lack of profitability', but that aside, in principle this is just a rent-to-rent structure.

You may also have heard of The Big Yellow Storage Company. Again, this is a similar model. They rent a big warehouse, they install storage units inside the warehouse to create lots of much smaller spaces and they let those spaces out for a monthly fee. This is what people are doing with rent-to-rent in the residential world now too. Many people think subletting is illegal. It isn't a crime, but it is a contractual issue. You will need the right contracts in place, the right insurances in place, the right communications in place - but I would say that is true for every business and it isn't too hard to get all of that sorted.

It is a brilliant business model when done properly, but it has its pros and cons. The most attractive pro is that it can generate a really high cash flow on a property that you didn't need to buy. You can get started much faster, with a much smaller pot and you can be making monthly cash flow in just a few weeks - no need for a mortgage, no need for a credit check, and no need for any of the complex form filling and valuations that go with buying houses. That being said though, you don't physically own anything, you are not building your net worth, you are simply running a business providing accommodation inside someone else's investment asset.

Depending on your own goals and objectives, this may not align. The other challenge with rent-to-rent is that you usually have to change the way a property is used, i.e., from a category C3 residential property to a category C4 HMO (House of Multiple Occupation). Those changes often need investment for full planning permission or at the very least, investment into the property itself, to adjust its fit-out to comply with standards. If you don't own the property, then you are investing money into someone else's assets, adding to their value and not your own.

Let me tell you how the numbers work on a rent-to-rent property so you can work out if this is a good business model for you or not. There are a few subcategories of rent-to-rent but for this scenario, I am going to focus on the rent-to-rent multi-let model, which is one of the most popular.

Let's take a four-bedroom, detached property with two reception rooms, a kitchen diner, one main bathroom, one ensuite and one downstairs toilet as a sample property.

You first take one of the reception rooms and make that a bedroom, so now you have five bedrooms and one reception room. You are creating a shared house also known as a House in Multiple Occupation.

Side note: If you are not in the property world yet, you might believe what you see in the media about HMOs and think HMOs are just grotty slum houses with bad tenants and scummy conditions, but times have changed. At the time of writing, this industry provides some of the most incredible, high-quality accommodation that is available.

OK, so you are creating a shared house. Those bedrooms, depending on location, could each rent out for approximately £650 per month = £3,250 gross rental income once full. Then you have your operating costs which are typically:

Utility bills - £200 a month

Broadband - £50 a month

Maintenance - £300 a month

Voids - £270 per month

Council tax - £200 per month

Insurance - £50 per month

TV Licence - £12 per month

Cleaning - £200 per month

Profit - £100 per room per month (£500)

So you offer to pay the landlord £1,468 a month, for up to 60 months, and you take responsibility for all of the moving parts of operating that property and all the people that stay there.

The landlord gets what they want, which is a consistent tenant on a long-term tenancy, often 5 years, no voids, one income source that is fully insured, a regularly cleaned and maintained property and a very hands-off approach to being a landlord. You, as the rent-to-rent operator, now control a property that you didn't have to buy and you are making £500 a month gross profit each month before tax and in-house operational costs. You would usually have to pay the first month's rent in advance, you will likely have to pay a deposit, and you would need to furnish the property for your residents and bring it up to standard, so you will need to have some funds to get started, but it is nowhere near what you would need to buy the house and get a mortgage on it.

You have probably heard of Airbnb. This platform changed the landscape of holiday lets and short-stay accommodation. Rent-to-rent works really well in this space too. You become the tenant in a two-bed apartment in central Manchester, for example. You pay the landlord £2,750 per calendar month but you can let the apartment out at £295 per night. You only have to have the apartment booked for seventeen nights of the month to break even and if you operate at 85% occupancy, you would make £1,339 per month profit after all costs, from a property you don't own, never had to buy or save up for. Can you see why people like this business model? When you compare it to average buy-to-let income, rent-to-rent becomes extremely attractive from a cash flow perspective.

Both of these business models, like every property business, are governed by compliance and legislation which you will want to study if you decide to go down this route. Some rent-to-rent arrangements will invalidate landlord insurance, be non-permissible under lease agreements, or could see a landlord breach mortgage terms, which means the property could be repossessed by the bank. However, when done correctly and with all of the correct measures, transparency and protections in place, you can see why people opt for this instead of actually buying property, especially in the early stages of property investing. You can make big money, really quickly, with very little start-up capital. The education company I started in 2018 specialises in helping Money Mechanics like you get started in property investing without the need for huge savings, just like I did. There is a really useful video about rent-to-rent available on this link. I invite you to check it out for more clarity. https://www.cogito-wealth.co.uk/r2r

Rent-to-Own / Tenant Buyer: This is one of my favourite property business models. I don't really understand why it is not more well-known and commonplace. It is a fantastic facility that allows people that wouldn't normally tick all the right boxes on a mortgage application to actively put themselves on the property ladder. It is more well-known in countries like Spain and with commercial property. In fact, at the time of writing this, I am in negotiations with a Spanish vendor to buy his eleven-bedroom, ten-bathroom, country farmhouse to convert into a retreat venue or rural entrepreneurs' getaway. When I asked the agent if the vendor was open to a rent-to-own offer, his answer was an immediate yes. I have also worked on acquisitions through rent-to-own in the UK and Canada over the past eight years and I have friends who have done this throughout Europe and America as well. It is really common in commercial property, however, it works in residential property just as well.

The wealthy know this, but many lower-income people have never heard of it or they assume it is not something they can do because they don't have money. You will probably think that to acquire a property you must buy it and have the money on day one to transact. The truth is that you don't!

If you are someone that has spent years thinking you will never own a house because you have been bankrupt, have lost a business, have been divorced, are old or any of the other reasons that mean you might not qualify for a mortgage, then this next section is for you!

Let's say you live alone, you are paying rent and you are trying to save a deposit but prices keep creeping up, making it increasingly difficult; maybe you went bankrupt in a previous life caused by poor management of money but you have fixed things and are back on track but you still don't tick the right boxes, or maybe you are in your late 50s or 60s and most mortgages will only offer you a 15-year term, so it pushes your monthly payments so high that it's simply impossible to buy a property. You can't take advantage of 100% mortgages because you are not a first-time buyer. If any of these situations sound like you, then you are who the tenant-buyer/rent-to-own business model is perfect for.

Rent-to-own is where the tenant rents a property from the owner for a specified length of time - in the UK, the limit is seven years (at the time of writing). The tenant has the option, but not the obligation, to purchase the property at a predetermined price point at some point during the term of the agreement.

Typically, the tenant pays a monthly rent, which should cover mortgage payments plus a 'top up' which goes towards the equity aspect of the purchase. Now, before I lose you, let me just explain that in most cases when you buy property you will have a mortgage (debt) and a deposit (equity). In the UK right now, for standard residential purchases, you can buy a house with 5-10% equity. There are 100% mortgages available but they are specifically for first-time buyers at the moment.

So, the 'top up' that the tenant-buyer pays is like a mini savings account that is chipping away at the purchase price of the property so that when the tenant-buyer comes to the stage where they are ready to buy, they don't need to have saved such a big deposit.

If you are a more visual person, like me, then I have broken the numbers down below so you can get your head around how this works.

Please remember these scenarios are for summary purposes only and every real life case would differ and be impacted by geographical differences in rents and interest rates.

Assumptions:

£250,000 property purchase price

Market rent is £1500 a month

Top up of £350 a month

Year 1:

Annual Rent Paid = £18,000 (1500 x 12)

Top Up = £4,200 (350 x 12)

Total = £22,200

Total Paid by the landlord towards the mortgage = £9,364.

The difference between the money received by the landlord as rent and money they have had to pay out to the mortgage company is £8,636 (landlord agrees to use 15% of this towards the purchase price).

Outstanding purchase balance = £250,000 (purchase price) - £4,200 (top-up) - £1,295.40 (15% of the rent) = **£244,504.60**

Year 2:

Annual Rent Paid = £18,000 (1500 x 12)

Top Up = £4,200 (350 x 12)

Total = £22,200

Total Paid by the landlord towards the mortgage = £9,364.

The difference between the money received by the landlord as rent and money they have had to pay out to the mortgage company is £8,636 (landlord agrees to use 15% of this towards the purchase price)

Outstanding purchase balance = £244,504.60 - £4,200 - £1,295.40 = **£239,009.20**

Year 3:

Annual Rent Paid = £18,000

Top Up = £4,200

Total = £22,200

Total Paid by the landlord towards the mortgage = £9,364.

The difference between the money received by the landlord as rent and money they have had to pay out to the mortgage company is £8,636 (landlord agrees to use 15% of this towards the purchase price)

Outstanding purchase balance = £239,009.20 - £4,200 - £1,295.40 = **£233,513.80**

Year 4:

Annual Rent Paid = £18,000

Top Up = £4,200

Total = £22,200

Total Paid by the landlord towards the mortgage = £9,364.

The difference between the money received by the landlord as rent and money they have had to pay out to the mortgage company is £8,636 (landlord agrees to use 15% of this towards the purchase price)

Outstanding purchase balance = £233,513.80 - £4,200 - £1,295.40 = **£228,018.40**

Year 5:

Annual Rent Paid = £18,000

Top Up = £4,200

Total = £22,200

Total Paid by the landlord towards the mortgage = £9,364.

The difference between the money received by the landlord as rent and money they have had to pay out to the mortgage company is £8,636 (landlord agrees to use 15% of this towards the purchase price)

Outstanding purchase balance = £228,018.40 - £4,200 - £1,295.40 = **£222,523**

What you have done is built in an equity pot of **£27,477** which can now be used towards the purchasing of the property. The market may also have adjusted upwardly in that five-year period. It could come down, of course, however, property trends typically increase when looked at over long-term periods. Even if the market has increased by just 15% then you have an additional pot of £37,500 built into the purchase at the point you actually transact. So, on a house you are buying for £250,000 you can use the equity you have built-in - totalling £64,977 in this scenario.

So, if you had purchased this property the traditional way, the figures look like this:

£25,000 deposit needed (on a 90% loan-to-value mortgage)

£1,500 legal fees saved

£0 Stamp Duty Land Tax (The threshold for this kicking in is £250,001 and would be 5% at the time of writing and in the UK - property taxes in other countries will vary. If you are a first time buyer the threshold is currently £425,000 in the UK)

And you would need a mortgage loan of £225,000 (90% loan to value) for typically 30 years which you would be paying 5.19% (today's typical rate) which is £1,234 per month.

If you used a rent-to-own method to buy the same home the figures would look like this:

£64,997 equity already in the agreement after five years

£0 deposit saved

£1,500 legal fees saved

£0 Stamp Duty Land Tax

And you would need a mortgage loan of £222,523 (77% loan to value) for typically 30 years which you would be paying 5.19% (today's typical rate) which is £962.42 a month.

When you use the creative acquisition method you will be paying less per month, and will have access to better mortgage products due to a lower loan to value requirement, as well as giving you the freedom to acquire the property sooner than you would have been able to by using the traditional method.

Now you might be thinking well, why would anyone sell their house like this?

There are lots of reasons but usually, it is to do with the motivation of the seller and the reasons they are selling. To be clear, not every seller will be able to consider this but many do if you actually ask them.

The seller will save on fees, they will spread the sale of their asset over a number of years which may have positive tax implications (I am not a tax advisor but some owners would see a saving in tax by selling in this way in the UK, at the time of writing), they get a steady monthly income with no gaps, from a tenant that is financially invested into the property and far more likely to look after it and keep on top of the maintenance and care of the property. This reduces the likelihood that you will stop paying rent, or fail to look after the property because if you do, you would forfeit your home purchase. Also, the owner achieves a committed sale, with a pre-agreed and contracted price, that they are happy with, with no costs of maintaining the property because the tenant-buyer takes responsibility for this from the point the agreement is signed, further reducing the burden on the owner. It really can be the perfect solution for many people.

There are, of course, contracts that need to be used. These are usually called 'Lease Options' or sometimes an 'Exchange With Delayed Completion', and if you embark on buying or selling a property using the rent-to-own/tenant-buyer model, then you certainly need to have a suitable solicitor that understands this creative property strategy to draw up and verify all of the right agreements. Most 'traditional' solicitors don't understand this because it isn't commonplace. My thoughts are that it absolutely should be. Imagine if generation rent could be buying the properties that thousands of landlords are trying to sell, using this property-buying hack. My belief is that the reason this is not more common is that the institutions don't really get much out of a partnership like this. The banks don't get their 'mort' (death) 'gage' (pledge), and the brokers and the money makers don't get paid. But now you know, you can start to find out more about this. Head to www.sarahpoynton.com/moneymechanicsresources and you will find more information about this there.

By understanding this, you may well be able to buy the home you are renting. Or, if you are a landlord trying to sell, you might want to ask your tenants if they would like to buy. Usually, both sides assume that buying/selling isn't possible but with this model, it may well be. I just wish more people knew how they could buy houses in this way. It would change the game for so many people!

Buy Refurbish Refinance Rent (BRRR): This is such a cool business model in property and is one of the most valuable when it comes to making your money go as far as it possibly can. This property investing model is where you purchase a property, then you add value to it in some way, then you refinance (change the mortgage/lending product) and rent it out. Let me break down these parts a little deeper.

We understand what buying a house is already. The biggest difference with this model is that instead of a mortgage loan, you take out the same amount of loan but usually from a different type of lender - usually referred to as a bridging loan - and then you also borrow some extra money to add value to the property.

Adding value means things like

- Renovations - new kitchens, bathrooms, flooring, ceilings, decoration
- Additional living spaces - extensions, loft conversions, adding bedrooms
- Landscaping - garden or patio area, creating a driveway
- Energy efficiency improvements - adding insulation, double glazing, solar panels
- Upgrading mechanical systems - electrics, plumbing, heating, HVAC
- Adding storage solutions
- Upgrading appliances and fixtures
- Reconfiguring the layout to create a different more valuable space to suit modern living
- Adding features that improve functionality - home office or gym
- Changing the use - turning a house into flats, creating an HMO

Some of these things are complex, but some of these are fairly simple and a beginner could certainly handle some of these without supervision or much hand-holding.

Once you have made the changes to the property and increased its value, you would then refinance off of your bridging loan onto a buy-to-let mortgage and then rent it out in the same way you would a simple buy-to-let.

When done well, this model allows you to recycle your money over and over again. Let me show you some numbers to make this make more sense.

Imagine a three-bed terrace property on the market. It is in poor condition and needs lots of work. You would be amazed how many homes there are like this, by the way.

The property is being sold for £180,000.

It needs £50,000 of work to bring it back to life.

Once it is renovated, it will be worth £300,000.

Let's look at how you make your money work in the best way and how this acquisition method is far more beneficial to your future wealth than typical buy-to-let.

25% deposit = £45,000

Legal Fees = £1,500

Valuation = £1,000

Stamp Duty = £5,400 (because this is usually a second property for most people, the rate is 3% of the purchase price).

So, you need £52,900 cash to start with.

The remaining £185,000 to buy and renovate the property, you would be borrowing from a bridging lender.

Then you complete the renovation. And now the property is worth £300,000.

But you don't sell it, you want to keep it. But leaving your £52,900 cash in the property isn't great for you because it is tied up, which means you can't add to your portfolio. You are stuck.

So, we need to get your money out (or as much of it out as we can). This is what you do.

You now Refinance. This is just a fancy word for moving the existing loan facility (your bridging loan) across to a standard buy-to-let mortgage. You replace one loan with another. But the exciting part of this is that now the property value is different from when you purchased it. The numbers look like this.

The value is now £300,000

You could potentially take out a 75% Loan-to-Value mortgage (subject to lender terms and applicable stress tests)

So, you get a mortgage for £225,000 from the lender.

You pay back the original loan of £135,000.

You pay back the refurbishment loan £50,000.

You would have paid interest on the borrowed funds of around 10% = £18,500

You are left with £21,500. Of the £52,900 cash you started with you have recovered £21,500. While you have left £31,400 in the deal it is actually an equity of £75,000 sitting in the property.

The profit that has been made from this project is £43,600. This profit is not cash in your bank, instead, it is equity in the investment. You are also left with a cash-flowing asset in your portfolio.

Flips A.K.A Buying-to-Sell: This is buying a house, adding value and then selling it and keeping the profit. It was made incredibly popular by TV shows like Homes Under The Hammer, which is still running here in the UK. I have clients that I have mentored through my education company, Cogito Wealth (www.cogito-wealth.co.uk), that have had property projects appear on Homes Under The Hammer.

Flipping houses is a fairly simple process to understand but it is not always easy to execute.

Just like with the B.R.R. model above, you have to find a property that you can add value to or this doesn't work. You need to look for property that needs modernisation, that has the potential to extend or reconfigure in some way.

Flips are for Money Mechanics that don't want to deal with tenants and don't want their money tied up for too long.

The best bits about flips are that you earn lumpy money. This is a term I coined in 2015 when I started in property. I was working on building portfolios for other investors and I was earning big lumps of money as a fee. I loved the idea of lumpy money because I am impatient and like to get to the result quickly. Lumpy money is big chunks of cash coming in in one go. With flips, the lumps of money can be huge. £10,000 is probably the lowest you would ever consider making on a flip, but the lumps of cash are uncapped. I know people doing two or three flip projects a year and making over £150,000 a time.

Let's say you buy a house for £230,000 and you can spend £100,000 on turning it into three flats. If each of those flats is valued at £150,000, you would make a profit of around £95,750 after all costs at the point you sold the flats. A project like that might take up to eighteen months. If you can't fund it yourself, you will have borrowing costs and other expenses like empty property holding costs (where you pay the council tax, gas and electric while it is empty), but still, it's a fantastic way to create wealth.

It seems simple but there are some hurdles and risks, as with anything we are talking about in this book. You have to decide which avenue or avenues match your risk profile.

The risks are that you buy a house you can't sell after the renovation, or you buy something having not understood the numbers correctly and it takes a lot more money to renovate than you anticipated, maybe there are delays or the materials costs shoot up as they did in 2020 and 2021. All of these things will chip away at your profits and if there are too many unexpected things, you could possibly lose money instead of making a profit.

In 2019, my business partners and I bought a property we were planning to flip. It was a dirty, smelly three-bed terraced house in Northampton. The plan was to flip it once we had finished it and we should have made around £40,000, after all costs, for around fifteen weeks of work. But right in the middle of the project, Covid happened. This meant that right when we were trying to sell it, agents were on lockdown, no one was answering the phone, and we couldn't get viewings organised... basically, we couldn't sell it. We had used investors' money to do this project and we had a looming repayment deadline. It was stressful, I won't lie, but in the end, we decided to pull funds from other places to pay back the investor and then keep the property and rent it out instead of selling it while we waited for everything to calm down in the market. We didn't get our £40,000 lump of money then, it had turned into a B.R.R. It turned out perfectly though, as now we still have that property and we have a net profit of £675 per month, on a three-bed terrace house. We have also built up around £80,000 of equity in that property as well, so the risk of not being able to sell it did come true for us on this one, but it worked out well in the end. When assessing a Flip, you will always want to consider a backup plan if it doesn't sell.

I hope I haven't blown your head up so far. The three business models above are amazing ways to make money from property. They all need some money to get started and for some of you, that is exactly the reason why you haven't got into property yet. So the next four things I am going to talk to you about is how you can make money from property without actually ever buying or renting a property. Then, in the last part of this chapter, I am going to explain to you how you can leverage other people's money so that you make an infinite return.

Portfolio Building A.K.A Property Sourcing: This is where I started in the world of property and creating financial independence. I wanted to make money from property but I had no money to buy property, or even rent it, so instead, I became a consultant. I learned how to identify a good investment from a bad one, I learned to understand risk and reward and I learned to connect with people that were looking at adding to their portfolios.

As a consultant, I would go out and hunt for the property based on the criteria they gave me. I would do all the negotiations with the vendors or in some cases, with the agents representing the vendors. I would secure the property at a price that worked for both sides and then I would make the introduction. The investor would move the investment forwards and once the contracts were completed, I got paid a fee for making that introduction. It was great. My only responsibility was to talk to people that were trying to sell or rent their properties and help them to find someone quickly that could buy or rent it from them - very similar to an estate agent but instead of being paid by the seller, I was paid by the buyer.

I would do all of the discovery conversations. I would ask what was driving the decisions and what they needed out of the deal in order to progress. I would then match them up with investors that I predominantly met through social media visibility. My average introducers fee was £3000 - £5000. My largest ever fee was £28,000, which was £1,000 less than my annual salary when I left my job. That was a multi-unit portfolio and so there was a small fee attached to each property in the portfolio. Once the buyer completed on them all, the total fee due to me was £28,000. The number of physical hours I worked on that transaction was probably around twenty hours. Twenty hours of calls, emails, proposals, communications, more phone calls and coordinating all the moving parts. It was hard work, it had to be accurate, however, when I compare that to the £29,000 basic salary I was paid in recruitment for 50 hours a week, every week, for a year, there really is no comparison. An hourly rate of £1,400. This is the sort of lumpy money that completely changed my world.

Now, for full transparency, these figures are turnover and not net profit. One of my absolute pet hates is when people say "I made six figures" when what they actually mean is they turned over six figures. In my world, net profit is what you "make". Turnover is just total sales. You can turnover £1,000,000 but if you spend £1,000,100 then you still lose money. The really impressive numbers are the net profit numbers. Anyway, I digress a little. All the money generated by the business was from property that I didn't own, while I had a terrible credit rating and I was £60,000 in debt.

Tell me again what is stopping you from starting to generate an income from property?

When I started this business in 2015, I had a failing business and I had a job doing sales and marketing consultancy work for another company to keep my bills paid. I launched and grew this property business from scratch, part-time, around lots of other commitments. I busted my butt, I am not going to sugarcoat it. I worked a lot. Maybe too much, with hindsight. I worked to the detriment of my health and my sanity at times, but I made it happen. I worked around the job and my other business. I tried to be a good wife and friend and aunty and everything else life brings our way.

I made every moment count. I would send messages to potential clients while I was walking from the office to my car, I would send emails while I was standing waiting for the kettle to boil. Most people who know me also know that I would always send text messages to new potential leads while I was having a wee. LOL probably TMI but that was the reality of it.

It didn't 'just happen'. I worked on relationships and learned how to identify good investments from bad investments so that I could personally benefit from helping other people to invest until I had the money to do it myself. I think this is the ultimate Money Mechanic, letting other people take the risk while you learn how to do it for yourself and get paid to do so. Work part-time, around your other income, until it replaces your income or you invest this additional income to generate other revenue. There is legislation surrounding this business model in different parts of the world, so if you choose to go down this route then be sure to research that. The full story of how I launched my portfolio-building business is available here https://www.cogito-wealth.co.uk/guide

REITS A.K.A Real Estate Investment Trusts: When I first heard about REITs, I was intrigued. As someone who loves real estate but didn't have never-ending capital to keep buying properties on my own, REITs offered a very interesting opportunity to invest in real estate without all the hassle. A real estate investment trust is a type of investment vehicle that owns and operates income-generating real estate properties. The REIT provides investors with a very diversified portfolio option, focused solely on real estate assets. But you can make money from a REIT without purchasing or managing a single brick yourself.

In the USA, REITs are required by law to distribute 90% of their taxable income to investors in the form of dividends; they are an extremely attractive option for investors seeking a regular income stream. I will talk to you about dividend income in much more detail when we get into the stocks and shares chapter, but for now, just know that dividends mean that you get paid in a passive way when you invest. REITs also have the opportunity for capital growth as the properties the REIT owns can appreciate over time.

In the UK, REITs are not required by law to distribute a certain amount of profits but to date, the trend is that they are distributing high percentages and sometimes they can be as high as is required in the USA.

There are two types of REITs - Equity REITs and Mortgage REITs.

An Equity REIT owns and operates income-producing properties such as office blocks, apartment blocks, residential estates and shopping centres.

A Mortgage REIT invests in real estate debt, such as mortgages and loans.

They are both traded on public stock exchanges, which makes them accessible to individual investors like you and I to invest in. All the assets are managed by the trust and the trust uses investors funds to fund growth. When you invest in a REIT, you become a shareholder and so you are paid an income linked to the size of your shares in the REIT.

There are risks of course. The housing market is volatile, like most markets, and economic conditions such as wars and pandemics can affect both the value of the assets owned and the income generated from them, which has a direct impact on the value of your shares and subsequently the amount you will earn.

What I love about them though, is that anyone can invest in real estate with as little as £10 or $10 or 10 Euros. They allow you to invest in a diversified, income-generating real estate portfolio that is entirely managed by someone else, and you get paid as a shareholder without any of the responsibilities of managing tenants, worrying about building work or the day-to-day impacts of the world around us. The income generated for you is passive and steady and comes in the form of a dividend. I love the idea that literally anyone can start to make money from property through a REIT with very little money. People ask me all the time "Can I really become a property investor with a tenner?" and the answer really is yes!

For those of you that have money, but absolutely no clue about property and no real desire to learn, you can become a property investor and let someone else handle the running of the portfolio and the choosing of the assets.

I invest in a few different ones and I won't name them here because I can't give you investing advice, but I can tell you that one pays me a 15.07% Dividend yield. I can tell you that around 3% of my whole investment portfolio is made up of investments in REITs.

This could be considered a great way to use your money to make money from property before you are in a position to actually buy your own. You absolutely have to do your due diligence, that goes without saying. Look for REITs in sectors you feel excited about.

There is a REIT for every industry - camping grounds, agricultural land, prisons, fancy hotels, care homes, billboards, medical cannabis... There is even one that owns and operates 1000 burger king and 55 Popeyes fast food locations. Find what you are interested in, look at the dividends that are paid and you can get started with as little as $0.53 for the lowest share in a REIT which is £RGL Regional Office REIT which pays 12.41% dividend yield (at the time of writing).

With the changes in landlord legislation (there are challenges globally) tax, tenant rights and more, it is becoming more and more common for landlords to be opting to leave property ownership completely and invest their funds into a very diversified REIT portfolio without any of the headaches. It is certainly very tempting on some days, I can't lie!

Crowdfunding: This has become a really popular way to invest in property since around 2015. It is a way to invest in large projects that are typically out of reach for low-income people. It is kind of like a big group of people pooling their resources to buy and add value to property assets, just like if a group of friends all chipped in to buy a holiday home, but with more legislation and better organised.

Previously, opportunities that needed large sums of money have only ever been available to super high net-worth individuals or institutional investors. Now, these projects are available to you! For example, a crowdfunding platform might present a hotel with planning permission to convert to a block of residential apartments. This project might be in the multiple millions to buy and even more millions to renovate it. Those sorts of projects are just in another league for most people. The crowdfunding platform facilitates getting investors' funds to the developer so the project can be realised. The same platform then facilitates the investor getting back their initial investment and the uplift that has been promised by the developer when the project has been completed. There are platforms that allow you to get started as a crowdfunding investor for as little as £1 initial investment. Crowdfunding is so accessible and considered to be one of the most secure ways of putting your money to work. Nothing is 100% risk free though!

One example of a property-specific crowdfunding platform is Property Partner. This platform allows investors to invest in residential properties in the UK and offers different types of investments, such as rental income shares, capital growth shares and development loans. Another example is CrowdProperty, which allows investors to fund loans to property developers in exchange for a fixed return on investment. I am not affiliated with any of these and these are not recommendations but simply a point in the right direction for you to start carrying out your own research.

These investments also carry risks. The property market is unpredictable and a property may not generate the returns or rents that were forecast. My advice is to do your due diligence on the platforms as your priority if you are starting to explore moving your money into crowdfunding. Not all platforms are made equal. Make sure you choose based on reputation and adherence to the strict regulations and rules that govern this sector globally. Make sure you choose a platform that provides you with really good due diligence on each opportunity so that you can choose your projects wisely.

Outside of the market and project risks, there are also credit risks. This is where the crowdfunding platforms lend the money out, but the borrower defaults.

They are insured and there is always contingency but as we saw happen in the 2008 financial crisis, if too many people default on loans all at the same time, a domino effect can cause huge impacts.

There are liquidity risks as well to consider, which is another reason to go with a reputable platform. Because they are not traded on the public market, the platforms are often illiquid. This means that they cannot be easily bought and sold if they ever got into trouble, which in turn, would make it hard for you to get access to your capital if you needed it back.

The last main risk to consider is the risk of the actual people operating the platform. Are they doing a good job? If they aren't and they went into insolvency, your funds would be lost, or delayed at the least. Choosing a reputable platform is the only way to mitigate this risk as much as possible, but it is never risk-free!

If what you want to achieve is an investment into real estate without needing thousands and without the headaches of actually becoming a developer to further diversify your portfolio, then moving your money into crowdfunding is a potential way to engineer a passive and low-risk income from the property market.

This chapter has dug quite deep into property and real estate. I hope you have learned that property investing is not out of reach for you. There are lots of ways to get involved in property. I have put a comparison table below to show you what the potential annual returns are on some of the options I have discussed based on a £20,000 investment. It is important to understand that these are examples only and are based on an assumption of a £20,000 investment over a 12 month period. Any investment could go down as well as up and so your capital is always at risk.

Investment	Initial Investment	Annual Yield	Annual Income	Risk Level
Buy-to-let	£20,000	4.75%	£950	Moderate to high
REIT	£20,000	15.03%	£3,006	Low to moderate
Crowdfunding	£20,000	15%	£3,000	High
Savings Account	£20,000	0.5%	£100	Low

Buy-to-Let is the most well known but it is not the lowest risk and it does not give you the highest returns on your money. These figures do not account for capital appreciation or leverage (which we discuss in the next chapter). However, they give you a really good visual to start considering if property is for you and if it is, which avenue could be for you based on your own objectives.

What do you think? Could property be for you?

Be sure to check out the Property Business Kickstarter training that is available on:

www.sarahpoynton.com/moneymechanicsresources

I have put together a free video training vault to help you understand these ideas even more!

CHAPTER 6

SHARE THE WEALTH: UNDERSTANDING STOCKS & SHARES AS AN INVESTMENT OPTION

I am really excited to write this chapter. Before I started learning about all of this, I thought that stocks and shares were things that only the super-rich played around with - something that you had to be super-rich to understand or be allowed to get involved with. I thought you had to go to stock exchanges like you see on the news or in the movies, you know, with all the craziness of people running around with bits of paper in their hands and looking very stressed. I thought that to become a stocks and shares investor, I would have to pass some kind of financial test with the banks and the companies that I wanted to buy shares in. You might laugh at this but I honestly thought stocks and shares were a "rich boys' club" thing and so I just didn't pay attention to them until I was in my mid-thirties. I didn't understand what a stock exchange really was. I didn't know the difference between a stock and a share and I had no idea how to make money in this space when I didn't really have that much to start with.

Now, I truly believe that the reason I (and probably you, as you are here reading this book) didn't understand any of these things is that no one in my world has ever invested in them. My school never taught me about this. My parents aren't investors. My grandparents had businesses and some investments but in true British style, never really talked about money openly. I was born in 1983 and up until 2017, I had never realised that someone like me was even allowed to invest in stocks and shares.

Now, some of you reading might think "What a wally" but that is the truth, that is how it was for me. I was actually a shareholder in my own business from 2012 and I still didn't make any connections.

You don't know what you don't know, right?!

So, when I started to understand stocks and shares better, to say I was very excited by their simplicity and accessibility is an understatement.

I wish someone had told me when I was eighteen that if I had taken £100 the day I turned 18 and invested it into stocks, averaging a return of 8% per annum (which is extremely realistic by the way, which I will explain shortly) and added just £25 a month until today (twenty-two years) that pot would now be worth £18,617. That is a deposit on a house in some areas of the world - not all, but some. It is university or college fees in some areas of the world. But no one ever explained this to me. We didn't talk about investments around the dinner table. We didn't talk about the markets. We never spoke about anything like this.

Now, I am surrounded by incredibly wealthy and successful people and one of the core things we talk about over dinner or drinks is money, investments, opinions, plans and ideas around money. There is a distinct lack of conversation in lower-income households around money and that is why most people do not know how to engineer their money to create wealth... yet!

We could hypothesise why the masses aren't educated on these things. We could say it is because the banks don't benefit from the masses being independent, or governments don't benefit from the masses being independent. I guess we will never really know the true answer to that question. These conversations about money, which would completely change the world, are kept as a 'secret' that only the wealthy know.

That is actually the whole reason I started to write this book because I want you to be financially independent so that every decision you make, everything you choose to do with your time, is chosen because you want to do it and not because you can't afford to make a different decision. I want you to have a life where your finances don't control your choices.

I know so many people that have stayed in toxic jobs, marriages and friendships because they couldn't afford to leave! For Money Mechanics, this can change!

So, let me lift the veil on this for you.

These are the main things that need answering:

1. What is a stock/share and what is the difference?
2. What are stock exchanges and the stock market?
3. What is a public vs private company and why should you care? What is an IPO?
4. What is a dividend and how do you earn it?
5. How much money do you need to buy stocks and shares?
6. Where do you go to buy stocks and shares?
7. What are the four different types of stocks and shares and which should you pick?

So, let's get into it.

The words stocks and shares are used interchangeably and it sometimes depends on where in the world you are. There are some very subtle differences.

If you are in the USA, you will usually refer to "stock" as ownership in a publicly traded company, whereas a "share" is used to refer to a unit of ownership in that stock. "I own Apple stock" or "I own 100 shares in Apple"

If you are in the UK, a "share" is used to refer to both ownership and units of ownership. "I own shares in BP" or "I own 100 shares in BP".

In most cases though, you can use them interchangeably and it will be correct and won't cause confusion. Moving forwards, I will use them interchangeably as well.

A share is literally when you own part of a publicly traded company. If you own a part of it then you are a shareholder and in many cases, this will mean you are entitled to a portion of its profits. Technically, as a shareholder, you also may have voting rights and a say in how the company is run, however, in big companies such as BP, where there are millions of shares, owning one or two isn't going to make your voice loud enough to make a difference.

The majority shareholders are the ones that are heard.

The next thing to understand is why a company would take itself public in the first place.

When a company goes public, what actually happens is that they sell shares in exchange for cash. On Initial Public Offering Day (IPO), the company issues shares and once an investor buying the shares pays for that share, that money permanently belongs to the company. They never have to pay it back, no interest is payable on the shares and there is no obligation to redistribute profits as dividends if they don't want to.

In the film, *The Wolf of Wall Street*, all about Jordan Belfort (a famous Wall Street trader), there is a part where Stratton Oakmont (Jordan's firm) takes Steve Madden Shoes public. In the initial offering engineered by Jordan, the company raised $11,000,000 by selling 1.8 million shares at $7 a share. That $11,000,000 remains in the business and can be used to grow, invest and improve. What is also quite cool is that the shares can then be traded between different investors, back and forth, and the company doesn't have any financial liability for them once sold. They do have a responsibility to keep shareholders happy through good performance, but that's it. If you haven't seen that film yet, I would recommend watching it but with an open mind and no children anywhere nearby! It does actually have some useful lessons in it about how the stock market works... Mostly lots about what not to do!

Other really famous IPOs that you might have heard of:

- Facebook in 2012 raised $16 billion, making it the biggest tech IPO in history at that point.
- Alibaba raised $25 billion in 2014, which set the record for the largest IPO in history
- In 2019, Uber raised $8.1 billion
- Airbnb raised $3.5 billion in 2020
- In 2020 Snowflake raised $3.4 billion

It is these initial public offerings that make the difference between public and private companies. A privately owned company retains control of its shares internally. A public company has its shares traded on the open (public) market.

Another really helpful thing to understand is what a stock exchange and the stock market actually is. This is something that felt like a bit of a mystery to me as well, before I really understood all this, so, let me explain this so you understand that this is a world you can get into very easily.

Imagine a giant outdoor farmers market or exhibition. It is full of traders from all walks of life. You can visit the market and you will find all sorts of vendors selling all sorts of different products - meat products, organic veg produce, soaps, tools and more. Now, within the farmer's market, there are sections where the organiser has grouped together similar product ranges, so all of the organic vegetables are found in one zone, all of the pet products are found in another zone, and all of the farm machinery is found in another zone.

A stock market is like a farmer's market and the stock exchanges are the zones within the market that group together different types of securities. A security is a collective name for stocks, bonds, index funds and more (which will all make sense by the end of this chapter, if it doesn't already).

OK, so you have the stock market (the whole market). It is made up of exchanges (zones) and in those exchanges, different securities (produce) are bought and sold. If an investor is looking to find a specific type of security they can go straight to the stock exchange that specialises in that security.

You may have heard of some of the exchange's names but never really known what they are. The most well-known are the London Stock Exchange, The New York Stock Exchange, The NASDAQ, The Shanghai Stock Exchange and The Japan Stock Exchange. There are plenty more but these are the most recognisable to people who are not embedded in the world of stocks and shares (yet!).

The next piece of the jigsaw puzzle is understanding the difference between a broker and a trader.

Allow me to use another metaphor. Have you ever been to a fancy cocktail bar? You know, the ones where instead of just ordering from a menu, the person serving the drinks asks you what you like and custom builds you a cocktail based on your own tastes?

Well, that person custom-making cocktails is called a mixologist. A mixologist is very different to a bartender, who is someone who takes an order and serves it to the customer in the best way possible.

A bartender is like a broker. They are there to facilitate what the customer wants. A stockbroker helps the customer to buy and sell securities. They facilitate the transactions. They usually charge a fee for their work in the form of a commission.

A trader is someone who is creating their own portfolio like a mixologist is creating their own drinks. They might create a unique mix of ingredients (securities) to achieve their goals. A trader is an individual or an institution that is buying and selling securities for their own account.

Now, you can't just become a broker. There is a load of legislation globally. You have to sit exams in most countries. It is a complex route... But ANYONE can be a trader - including you!

A trader is someone that buys and sells securities for their own account. The second you understand that being a trader or an investor is not something that only wealthy, qualified, highly-educated people can do, then the game changes for you. Now you have access to the same stock market and the same stock exchanges and, in many cases, the same stock brokers that the super-rich use, but you can get started with £10 or $10 or 10

Euros and you can do it from your own phone or laptop, at home.

Now, a bit of transparency here, I wouldn't call myself a trader. I would classify myself as an investor. For me, investing in stocks and shares is a long-term play. Typically, when I buy a share of something, my intention is to hold it long-term. Long-term in my world means I am likely to hold those securities for five years or more unless something significant occurred in the markets. A trader is someone that buys and sells - sometimes on the same day, sometimes weeks later, sometimes months later, but the intention is to buy, wait for it to increase in value and then sell it to make a profit.

An investor, on the other hand, generally has a buy and hold strategy behind them. I am in that camp. The reason for that is because of compound interest. I am going to break down compound interest and leverage separately in their own chapter because they are so cool and really the lynchpin that holds together future financial independence, so they need their own chapter.

The point here is that YOU can become an investor, or trader, or both, immediately. You don't need any special equipment, you don't even need to understand all those funny charts and the squiggly lines of red and green boxes. You can set up an account on something like Freetrade, which is the one I use, though there are lots of others, and you can transfer £10 or $10 or 10 Euros to your account and buy your first share in seconds.

In fact, if you use this link to join Freetrade

https://magic.freetrade.io/join/sarah/31b2d84f

and top up £50 into your account then Freetrade will actually give both you and I a share worth between £10 and £100 as a sign up bonus. Being given a share for free is zero risk, so a really great way to learn.

Some of the other platforms that exist are listed below. They all make it really easy with an app on most smartphones:

- Hargreaves Lansdown
- Trading 212
- Etoro
- Interactive Investor

These are not the only ones but you can get started here. Platforms like these have made it easy for Money Mechanics like us to access the same money-making tools that the wealthy have had access to for years. Now you can join the party.

If you are one of those people who know they want to get started, then go and choose yourself a platform, top up your account with just a little bit, an amount you can afford to lose - £10, £20, £50 - then pick a stock and buy it. I will say here that it is always important to understand that there are risks associated with any investing. I would encourage you to read the risk warnings found later in this chapter before you dive in.

Buying stocks is obviously a really personal thing and let's be honest, if you are someone that has absolutely no bloody idea what they are doing (me, circa 2019), then here are some ideas that might just help you get out of your own way and get started.

First of all, I like to think about what I consume. I have shares in lots of the things that I personally use: Apple, Google, BP, Zoom, Meta (Facebook), Coca-Cola, Amazon, Easy Jet, Coinbase and Colgate Palmolive to give you examples. These are all companies I buy products or services from. I remember scrolling through the list and there was confidence in recognising the names for me. I knew what they did. I buy from them so clearly I have faith in what they do. When I first started out I started there. I bought shares in companies I knew.

Over time, I learned that there are four different types of shares that you can buy.

- Defensive stocks - As the name would suggest these are the types of companies that are considered stable and secure. Long-standing, defensive. They are called defensive because whilst they don't give crazy good returns, they are the 'old faithful'.

Here is a list of some companies that are typically called 'defensive':

- Procter & Gamble Co. (PG)
- Johnson & Johnson (JNJ)
- Coca-Cola Co. (KO)
- PepsiCo Inc. (PEP)
- Walmart Inc. (WMT)
- McDonald's Corp. (MCD)
- Nestle SA (NSRGF)
- Colgate-Palmolive Co. (CL)
- AT&T Inc. (T)
- Verizon Communications Inc. (VZ)
- Southern Co. (SO)
- Duke Energy Corp. (DUK)
- Dominion Energy Inc. (D)
- Public Service Enterprise Group Inc. (PEG)
- NextEra Energy Inc. (NEE)

The letters in brackets next to each are its ticker symbol. These are the letters that are used to identify a stock on the exchange.

The classification as 'defensive' can change over time based on market conditions and industry performance. It is important to recognise that past performance is never an indication of future results and they all come with risk.

- Growth Stocks - These are the types of stocks that are often unknown but considered to have the capability of growing and increasing in value at a faster rate than everything else in the market. Growth stocks can be volatile, but not always. Sometimes they are considered growth because they hold a monopoly in a market, like Right Move or Apple. That said, Apple, in the last twelve months, has started to lose its hold on the market and has actually shredded $1 trillion off of its market cap during 2022.

Here is a list of stocks that are considered "growth stocks", taken from a Forbes article by Jo Groves and Andrew Michael in March 2023:

- Apple (AAPL)
- Rightmove (RMV)
- Denali Therapeutics Inc (DNLI)
- Moderna Inc (MRNA)
- Netflix Inc (NFLX)
- Planet Fitness Inc (PLNT)
- Schroder Big Society Capital Social Impact Trust (SBSI)
- Team17 Group PLC (TM17)
- Zytronic plc (ZYT)

As with defensive stocks, the classification evolves and so it is important to do further research before committing to any one stock. **DIVERSIFICATION is EVERYTHING!** There is a section later in this chapter that explains the golden rule of diversification in more detail.

- New Issue Stocks - Now, we have actually already talked about these, when I explained earlier what an Initial Product Offering was, an IPO. Remember Steve Madden Shoes in The Wolf Of Wall Street? That is what a new issue stock is. It is a stock that is coming to the market for the very first time. There are lots of these. In fact, as I am sitting here writing this chapter, it is a very sunny April in 2023 and so far this year, there have been fifty-one IPOs on the US stock market alone. There is never a shortage of IPOs to get involved with.

Here is a list of anticipated IPOs for 2023:

- Mobileye
- Stripe
- Vinfast
- Databricks
- Reddit
- Discord
- Instacart
- TikTok
- Chime
- Epic Games
- Fanatics

There are definitely some companies on here that I am a customer of and with my rule of "invest in what you consume or know", I will certainly be keeping an eye out for when the dates are announced.

- Dividend Stocks - This is the fourth and probably my personal favourite. I shared at the start of this chapter that when you become a partial owner of a company, in some cases, you are paid a passive dividend as a shareholder. Well, these are the companies that pay you a dividend as a shareholder. Not all companies that you buy stocks in will distribute profits, but some do and when they do, you get paid passively straight into your account. True passive income! You get paid, for as long as you own shares and for as long as the company is distributing profits.

Here is a list of dividend stocks and what dividends they currently pay in 2023:

- AT&T Inc. (T) - Dividend yield: 5.57%
- Verizon Communications Inc. (VZ) - Dividend yield: 6.65%
- Exxon Mobil Corp. (XOM) - Dividend yield: 3.14%
- Chevron Corp. (CVX) - Dividend yield: 3.50%
- Pfizer Inc. (PFE) - Dividend yield: 3.98%
- Coca-Cola Co. (KO) - Dividend yield: 2.92%
- Procter & Gamble Co. (PG) - Dividend yield: 2.49%
- Johnson & Johnson (JNJ) - Dividend yield: 2.73%
- IBM Corp. (IBM) - Dividend yield: 5.15%
- Ford Motor Co. (F) - Dividend yield: 4.79%

If you look at the table below, it shows you the annual income you would earn if you owned £500 of each of these dividend stocks

Stock Name	Dividend Yield	Investment (£500)	Annual Passive Income
T&T Inc. (T)	5.57%	£500	£27.85
Verizon Communications Inc. (VZ)	6.65%	£500	£33.25
Exxon Mobil Corp. (XOM)	3.14%	£500	£15.70
Chevron Corp. (CVX)	3.50%	£500	£17.50
Pfizer Inc. (PFE)	3.98%	£500	£19.90
Coca-Cola Co. (KO)	2.92%	£500	£14.60
Procter & Gamble Co. (PG)	2.49%	£500	£12.45
Johnson & Johnson (JNJ)	2.73%	£500	£13.65
IBM Corp. (IBM)	5.15%	£500	£25.75
Ford Motor Co. (F)	4.79%	£500	£23.95

Now you are not going to retire on £23.95 a year. There are some stocks that go much higher than this, but I want to bring you a balanced viewpoint on all this. I have some of my own dividend stocks that pay much higher than these at 8.25%, 7.23%, and 15.50% in some cases.

When you get started, especially if you are starting with small amounts, then it can feel a little pointless making an extra £23.95 a year, but when you read the chapter on compound interest and how these tiny amounts grow over time, you will wish you had started sooner.

In everything you do in the stock market, there is always a risk associated. The main aspects of risk you need to consider are

Market Volatility - The stock market can be volatile and the prices and values of stock can fluctuate significantly based on what is happening in the world. Political events, technology and innovation, regulatory change, released earnings reports, economic indicators and monetary policy - all of these things are likely to move the market up or down. Many of these things are unpredictable. No amount of research will be able to prepare you for if there is a pandemic, for example.

There is risk associated with the specific company. Poor management conditions, competitive pressures, legal issues and financial performance will all impact share prices. You have no control over these things but the value of your investments is directly impacted by them.

Liquidity Risk - Liquidity is the ease with which an asset can be converted into real cash without the market value being impacted. The stock market can be illiquid, meaning that it could be difficult to sell stocks quickly during times of market volatility.

Inflation risk - This exists because inflation is eroding the buying power of your money as it increases, which does have an impact on the value of the returns you are gaining from the market over time.

Interest rates - You probably won't have considered it but the value of stocks is directly impacted by the company's profits. If the company has debt, the costs of borrowing that money will go up when interest rates go up. This means profits will inevitably come down. In contrast, if interest rates come down, it stimulates economic growth and increases performance and demand for stocks.

Systemic, political and regulatory risk - This is everywhere and these things have a direct impact on the value of your investments. There is often sudden unexpected disruption caused by the people in power making poor decisions or communicating them poorly to the masses. A perfect example of this was the 'mini-budget', as it has been dubbed, that came from Liz Truss during her 'five minutes' in Number 10 Downing Street in 2022. It is a prime example of a political communication that was delivered poorly, rushed through and did not consider the repercussions that impacted the market drastically.

There are always going to be potential risks of investing in stocks and shares but on the flip side there is always going to be potential for growth and so you have to always balance risk and reward and remember **DIVERSIFICATION is EVERYTHING!**

What do I really mean when I say diversification?

Before I really started learning about all this stuff, I knew what the word meant, like the literal translation made sense to me. Don't put all your eggs in one basket! But how to actually make that a reality I couldn't get my head around when I first started. It was another one of those words that overcomplicated things in my brain.

All that is meant by a diversified portfolio is that you spread your investments across different companies and also different industries, different asset classes and different risk levels.

When you diversify, you are hedging against failure in one part of your portfolio. It means that if one industry suffers a hit the rest of your portfolio is ring-fenced (to an extent) from those changes. This is the best way to protect your interests for the long term.

If you create a portfolio that is like a pick-n-mix bag with a really good mixture, and you regularly increase the number of sweets in your bag, then you are going to consistently be moving towards your financial independence position.

The last thing I imagine you are still thinking about is how much money you should invest, when should you invest, and how do you time it right. How do you know that you will be doing the right thing?

That sounds like a tough set of things to work out right?

Ultimately, you do not know the future, none of us do. And unless you are a very well-educated experienced trader that understands those charts and wiggly lines, then trying to time the market right is as good as impossible. Don't even bother!

Trying to time the market perfectly is also just loads of hard work. I am not a fan of making things hard for myself when it can be quite simple. Instead of trying to time the market, what a Money Mechanic does is automate their investing.

The way I do this is by using a tactic that most people have never heard of, called dollar cost averaging. When I learned about this, it took so much pressure off me trying to choose the right thing on the right day at the right price. My life is complex enough, I don't need the extra pressure and I bet you don't either. So, this is what I do instead.

All you have to do is buy the same amount, of the same stock, on the same day each month regardless of the price. That is right, don't worry about the price.

You have twelve months in a year. Imagine you have £25 a month available to invest. Instead of checking the charts every day and trying to get in on the right day every month, all you have to do is buy £25 of the shares you have chosen on the first of the month, every month (or a date that works for you). In some months, you might get three shares for your £25, in other months, you might get five shares for your £25 and in other months, you might get one share for your £25. But this strategy of buying the same dollar/pound amount on the same day every month has been proven to actually create higher returns for the investor over time.

Sometimes the cost is higher, sometimes it is lower but as an average over the year, you will end up with more bang for your buck. Automating your decisions also takes the emotions out of it and you end up with a portfolio that is less affected by short-term market fluctuations.

I set up a direct debit from my bank account on payday, it goes straight to my Freetrade account, and I go in and I split my pot up. I buy the same amount of each of my shares every month. I also roll my dividend payouts back into my investments, so even if I have a £0.01 dividend one month from a stock that I own (I got this from ESG Global (Dist) in March 2023), I roll that back into buying shares. This means that every month I have just that little bit more to go into my future wealth creation pot.

I don't have to think about it, I don't have to study markets, I don't have to understand the charts and I don't need to worry about the fluctuations, but when I look back after year one, year two and beyond, I can see my wealth increasing and my ROI increasing. I have put my passive income back to work, which is giving me infinite returns because it was free money (in my mind). This is the sort of Money Mechanic life that I am here for. Complex investing activity is simply not for me.

You might be wondering why I haven't talked about when to sell.

The reason for that is that this book is about Money Mechanics and how to actually engineer your money to create future wealth. Buying and selling is trading and it does mean you need to time things right. It can be done, of course, but if you sell a share, you don't own it anymore and so the cash is back with you and cash in the bank is dead money.

If you want to engineer your money for the future then selling isn't really what you will want to do. Most inexperienced people sell when the markets are coming down because they panic, but that is the opposite of what you will want to do. Warren Buffet famously said, "When others are greedy be fearful, when others are fearful be greedy". When inexperienced investors panic sell because of market movements, what they are doing is crystallising a loss a lot of the time. Then they say "I lost loads of money in the stock market". The truth is that as long as you still own the asset (share) then you haven't lost money, it has just changed in price. If you sell because you are panicking then you are likely to lose money. You have to hold your nerve and stick to the plan, which is that we are Money Mechanics and we are engineering our money for the future. We are playing the long game!

When all of these things are combined you can move confidently forward as an investor in the world of stocks and shares. When your automated, unemotional, stress-free efforts today turn into financial abundance in ten, fifteen, or twenty years, you will be grateful to your current self for being brave and getting started. Even if you are starting with £10, £50 or £100, it all makes a huge difference.

CHAPTER 7
A WEALTH OF OPTIONS: NAVIGATING ETFS, MUTUAL AND INDEX FUNDS

I f you can imagine that investing in a stock of one company is like buying a single stem flower, then investing in a fund is like buying a whole bouquet of flowers.

You are learning all through this book, the importance of diversification and finding ways to de-risk your money so that it can build over time. In my opinion, fund investing is one of the most powerful ways to diversify your portfolio, especially as a beginner. At the start, the whole process of choosing companies to buy shares in is daunting and sometimes overwhelming enough that it may just stop you dead in your tracks.

Funds are a tool that can take the pressure off because a fund means you are buying shares in a collection of companies and not just one. You are naturally diversifying.

There are three main types of funds:

An index fund

A mutual fund

An exchange-traded fund

In this chapter, I am going to help you understand the difference and show you how you get going with the one that is best for you. Even if you are starting with under £100 or $100 or 100 Euros.

Let me first explain what a fund is in really simple terms. I used the analogy of a bunch of flowers earlier. A bunch of flowers has many stems, many flower heads and many petals. When you buy a bunch of flowers, you are not relying on one single flower. If one flower in a bunch of flowers wilts a little, the rest of the bunch of flowers will still look fantastic.

Well, this is just like an investment fund.

When you invest in a fund what you're actually doing is buying a tiny part of lots of different companies.

The S&P 500 (Standards & Poors 500) is the USA's largest 505 companies. It is a fund that tracks the performance of all of those 505 companies. So instead of you having to independently go and buy shares in each of those 505 companies to diversify your investments, you can invest in the fund. You simply buy a share in the S&P 500 fund and you own a tiny part of all 505 companies.

The FTSE 100 (Financial Times Stock Exchange) will be the one that most UK people recognise. It's a fund that tracks the largest 100 companies in the UK. When you buy a share in the FTSE 100, you are investing a tiny amount in each company on the list.

There is a long history when it comes to funds. Mutual funds, index funds and ETFs all have their place, but for Money Mechanics like us, for people that want to keep life simple and take the complex thinking out of becoming wealthy, as I learned more and more about this topic I realised that *my* preference is an index fund. Let me tell you why.

Mutual funds began life back in the 1920s. They were a way for wealthy men to pool their money to invest in a diversified group of securities. Over time, they became really popular as a way for investors to gain access to diversified portfolios. A mutual fund is actively managed by a fund manager. Because of this, they are often expensive and when you invest with them, they typically charge high fees and commissions, which will erode the investors' returns. In my experience, most mutual funds charge a management fee of around 2% per year and then on top of that, they retain 25% of your profit leaving you with 75%. That is how they get paid for the service of improving your wealth.

In 1976, John Bogle, the founder of the Vanguard Group, identified that most mutual funds were not outperforming the market over the long term. He believed that a fund that simply tracked the performance of a market would be a better option for investors because it wouldn't need to be actively managed. This meant that investors could be saved from the expensive fees and profit splits that mutual funds demand. He created the first index fund, the S&P 500, which has since become one of the most effective, low-cost ways for investors of all levels to gain exposure to the stock market without having to really understand the stock market. Perfect for Money Mechanics like us who are just getting started.

Index funds have become a very popular option thanks to the evolution of tech and because they are not actively managed. They are my favourite option because they basically take all of the thinking out of investing in the stock market. You simply enter and the fund does the rest of the work, but, unlike a mutual fund, the costs are lower and so as investors, we are able to retain more of our wealth.

A mutual fund attempts to outperform the market. An index fund simply tries to match it.

An exchange-traded fund (ETF) works in a really similar way but they track a specific market index.

They all have their place. Mutual funds, however, are often inaccessible to the masses because you have to invest a minimum of £50,000, £100,000, and sometimes, over £1,000,000 to be considered a worthy investor, whereas I can go to Freetrade and buy into the Vanguard S&P 500 with £61.98 (the price on the day I am writing this) and buy one share. That makes me an investor. You can easily do the same.

An index fund is typically much more accessible to Money Mechanics like us.

When it comes to investing in funds there are different strategies.

- Buy and hold
- Dollar cost averaging
- Sector rotation
- Asset allocation (and tactical allocation)

I am not going to blow your heads up explaining all of these. As I said at the start of the book, my ambition is to share with you what I do and what I believe, in my opinion, to be the path of least resistance when it comes to getting started towards your financial independence.

I think that combining 'buy and hold' with 'dollar cost averaging' over the long term will create financial independence and eventually complete financial freedom. You can learn about the other strategies later if you want to, but don't overcomplicate this for now. The reason most people don't get started working on their financial independence through investing is that they overthink it and over complicate it to start with. Don't get stuck in that place.

If you take the S&P 500, for example. Over the past thirty years, it has delivered a compound average annual growth rate of 10.7% per year.

That means if you took £100 today and added £20 a month to the account using dollar cost averaging and an average of 10.7% per year, you would have invested £2,500 of your own money in 10 years, but you would have earned an extra £2,055.40 in interest. A total value of £4,555.40.

If you carried on that trend for fifteen years your pot would be £9,337.42

If you carried on that trend for twenty years your pot would be £17,483.13

And just to show you what happens if you start at eighteen and leave it until you are sixty-five, based on £100 initial capital and just £20 a month your pot would be worth £347,829.28 at sixty-five.

£11,380 would be your money and you would have earned £336,449.28 in interest.

The greatest part about being in a fund like the S&P 500, is that you are automatically diversified.

I have stated the importance of diversification multiple times and I will say it again more than once before this book is finished. Diversifying your portfolio is so important but sometimes this can be overwhelming. Hunting for the right blend of stocks, figuring out the details enough to choose a stock, wading through all the jargon and figuring out which industry is doing what... it is a lot to get your head around. If you are anything like me, you want all the spoils of a diversified investment portfolio without all the brain work. Who has really got the time?

A fund gives you simplicity and diversification. Just like with a bunch of flowers, you own a small share of every single petal (company) in that fund. This matters because if one fails or doesn't perform, there are all of the others to take up the slack. That will give you and your money some protection. Every year there are reshuffles and some companies exit and some enter the funds.

If you take the FTSE 100. In September 2022, there were three companies that were victims of the reshuffle. Abrdn, Hikma Pharmaceuticals and Howden Joinery Group. Now I don't know about you, but I had only heard of one of those companies (Howden), but I have been invested in all of them through the FTSE 100 investments that I hold. You see, you could be making money from companies you have never even heard of when you choose index funds. How cool is that?!

The three companies above were axed because they were all down 40% and deemed to be underperforming. They were replaced by ConvaTec Group, F&C Investment Trust and Harbour Energy.

If you were investing in specific stocks, you would have to be on top of what every single stock is doing and its performance. You would have to have your eye on the ball. When you opt to go down the route of an index fund, that is all done for you and you have the protection of the other companies in the index fund to keep you incredibly well diversified.

You are probably guessing I love index funds. They are hands-off. I invest the same amount each month into the same index funds and I just sit back and let them build over time. For me personally, they work.

That being said I promised you a balanced view on everything so it is important to talk about the disadvantages of index investing. The first is that you don't have control of the downside protection. There is no floor to losses which means there is no limit to how much money someone can lose. There is no guarantee that the markets will perform in the future the way they have in the past.

If you took £100 and you put it into the S&P 500 today and tomorrow the market dropped by 50%, then the value of your investment would have halved, in theory, 'losing' 50% of your money. There being no floor to losses means that the downside has no limit. It is important to remember what I have mentioned previously, that you only really lose money if you panic sell in a down market. Selling an asset for less than you bought it for is a surefire way to crystallise a loss. Money Mechanics don't panic sell in a bear market!

Money Mechanics understand that there is a risk of volatility and that the value of your investments will go up and down in waves over time and that is ok. That is how it is supposed to be. That is why we diversify to mitigate those risks.

Another disadvantage of index investing is that you have no choice over the fund's composition. You cannot remove or add any securities. You are buying into a set bundle. Let's say that you are a very socially responsible or health-focused investor and you would never want to profit from a tobacco company out of principle. In that case, you couldn't invest in the FTSE 100 because inside of that fund sits Imperial Brands. Imperial Brands owns Golden Virginia, Davidoff, Lambert & Butler, West and Rizla. When you invest in an index fund you take a tiny amount of shares in all of the companies within it. There are no index funds (at the time of writing) that exclusively contain ethical and socially responsible companies within them because index funds are designed to track a market index. However, there are a number of mutual funds and ETFs that focus on ethical and socially responsible companies.

Here are a few of them if this is a direction you may want to go:

1. Vanguard ESG U.S Stock ETF - this tracks the performance of the FSTE US All Cap Choice Index which includes companies that meet certain environmental, social and governance criteria
2. iShares MSCI KLD 4000 Social ETF - which includes companies with positive ESG characteristics
3. Calvert Equity Fund (CSIEX) invests in companies that meet certain social and environmental criteria and has a specific focus on sustainability and climate change

These are a few examples but as I have said throughout this book, it is important to do your research. I am not recommending these. I don't personally invest in any of these. I wanted to show you that whatever your personal criteria for choosing a place to invest, there are options available to you.

The third disadvantage of index investing is that you cannot beat the market. Index funds have a specific intention and that is to match the market. If you are looking for investments that beat the averages of the whole market then index funds will not be right for you. A mutual fund or ETF can beat the market but an index fund cannot.

My take on that though is that 10.7% per year on average, compounded over time in a fee-free and commission-free way, without me having to give much head space to it, feels like a great layer to a really positive and diversified portfolio.

I have talked about the S&P 500 and the FTSE 100 because I personally like them and invest in them. I chose them after doing some research and understanding it a little bit more than having absolutely no clue.

There are a few ways that you can do some digging if you want to. The first thing that will impact your fund choice will be your own investment goals. For example, those of you reading this that want to invest with high risk for high rewards and have a target of generating 30% per year (which is possible, but riskier) would never choose the S&P 500 because it will likely never return that money, based on past performance. Knowing your objectives will help you choose by a process of elimination.

You can compare the past performance of different funds as well. You can usually find performance data on websites such as the Financial Times or Morningstar. By looking at the fund's returns over several years, you will get a good sense of which one works for you. Always bare in mind that your research into past results is a guideline only and not a guarantee of future performance.

Another thing to look at is the fees and expenses associated with any particular fund. Those pesky fees all add up and can actually eat quite heavily into your profits over time. You can find a prospectus online about most funds and they have to be transparent about the fees and expenses. Funds with lower expense ratios are going to cost you less. A prospectus will also outline the fund's individual risk strategy and other operational details that could help you decide. For full transparency, I am a big-picture person and I don't get into really deep detail so I haven't read many fund prospectuses. I just stick to index funds rather than actively managed ETFs or mutual funds. I have received fund prospectuses and as I read them, I realise that I am happy where I am. This may change over time but I am a simple creature and my brain is so full up running my businesses that filling up my brain with more detail about investing would be distracting. One of my core investing 'must haves' is simplicity. I don't like to think too much about it. I am a Money Mechanic with a desire for simplicity and automation.

You have to choose your own path aligned with your personal investment objectives.

The most important thing is to choose something!

Learning everything in this chapter and doing nothing about it would be madness.

You are a Money Mechanic now, so go and get started and watch the markets do all the heavy lifting!

CHAPTER 8

COMPOUND INTEREST: THE SILENT GIANT OF WEALTH ACCUMULATION

O K first of all let me just say that you are doing great. Up until now, we have really dug deep into some quite complex topics. It took me years to unravel the complex topics we have talked about so far and you are absorbing them really quickly, so, a little salute from me to you. You are doing great!

This chapter is going to help you get your head around the importance of thinking long-term when it comes to your Money Mechanics.

First, let's talk about compound interest.

Albert Einstein said "Compound interest is the eighth wonder of the world. He who understands it earns it, he who doesn't, pays it."

In the earlier chapter about debt, we talked about how credit card companies make their money. They are earning it and you are paying it. Many credit cards compound interest on a daily basis.

This chapter is going to show you how you can start building your wealth using the same techniques that the credit card companies, the banks, and the super wealthy are using because it is actually available to everyone!

Fancy a bit of that?

This stuff blew my mind when I started learning about it. I have always assumed that to be able to make the sorts of returns the super-rich were making, I had to have the same amount of money. I thought I had to be a multimillionaire and then I could start investing and living a life where my money was making more money. But this couldn't be further from the truth. You don't have to be rich to start investing, starting to invest is what will make you rich! The main ingredient of being able to truly benefit from compound interest is **TIME.**

Compound interest is where you earn interest on your initial money invested and then you also earn interest on the accumulated interest that you make daily, weekly, monthly and yearly.

Compound interest is interest earned on your interest.

This causes the value of your investment to grow at an increasing rate over time.

There is a formula for this:

$A = P(1 + r/n)^{(nt)}$

A = is the future value of the investment or loan, including interest

P = is the initial principal (the original investment or loan amount)

r = is the annual interest rate (as a decimal)

n = is the number of times interest is compounded per year

t = is the number of years

Now you know the formula you can go ahead and forget it because there are calculators online, including one on my website www.sarahpoynton.com/moneymechanicsresources, that work this stuff out for you.

Compound interest is one of the most amazing aspects of investing but one of those things that is never explained to us in simple terms and so, for many 'non-investors', it feels complex and something that is out of reach for them. Compound interest is what will make you wealthy if you stick to the Money Mechanics rules.

The longer you are in the market and the more frequently the interest is compounded, the greater the growth of your personal wealth.

So let's look at some numbers. I want to give you a few scenarios that I believe are available to most people.

First, I want to talk to all the parents. I am not a parent and won't even try to say I understand the financial struggles that come with being a parent. The cost of childcare is crazy high and everything a child needs is expensive. I am told that they eat everything in sight until the day they leave home. For normal income households, keeping on top of the cost of children is expensive. All parents have something in common though, right? You all want to provide the best life possible. The best you can with what you have. What if there were a way to set your children up for financial success and independence in their twenties by starting small from the day they were born?

There is a way and this is something that is commonplace in wealthy households, but in most middle and low-income households this just does not happen and it doesn't happen because no one has ever told you how. That is why I wrote this book, so that you can create financial independence for yourself and the generations that follow!

From the day we are born until the day we turn twenty-five, there are 300 months.

When a child is born most babies get gifts and clothes and books and teddies and loads of really cute things. Every family is different and of course, and the budget for these things change based on available funds.

Then they all have twenty-five birthdays, twenty-five Easters and twenty-five Christmases.

So, let's assume that on each of those occasions, an 'investment budget' of £25 could be syphoned off to a separate pot. You could maybe forgo one of the gifts you would normally buy, or ask relatives to all chip in a few pounds each to make up the £25, instead of buying a bigger gift. If you communicate what you want and why you are doing this, most people will be more than willing to adjust the way they contribute gifts to help create financial independence in the future life of this child.

So we have

Twenty-five birthdays = £625

Twenty-five Christmases = £625

Twenty-five Easters = £625

Welcome to the World gifts £25

A total of £1,900.

If you put that into a savings account, your returns would be low over twenty-five years, meaning that on their twenty-fifth birthday, you could only hand them around £1,900.

But what if you did this instead?

An initial investment amount of £25.

Followed by an additional £75 (3 x £25) per year contributed to the pot.

Invested at an average of 10% per annum (which, as we now know, is fairly low risk in something like the S&P 500), this would give an account worth £8,220 on their twenty-fifth birthday.

The table below shows how this actually works and you will see how compound interest makes such a difference.

Year	Deposits & Withdrawals	Interest	Total Deposits & Withdrawals	Accrued Interest	Balance
0	£25.00	–	£25.00	–	£25.00
1	£75.00	£2.62	£100.00	£2.62	£102.62
2	£75.00	£10.75	£175.00	£13.36	£188.36
3	£75.00	£19.72	£250.00	£33.09	£283.09
4	£75.00	£29.64	£325.00	£62.73	£387.73
5	£75.00	£40.60	£400.00	£103.33	£503.33
6	£75.00	£52.71	£475.00	£156.04	£631.04
7	£75.00	£66.08	£550.00	£222.11	£772.11
8	£75.00	£80.85	£625.00	£302.96	£927.96
9	£75.00	£97.17	£700.00	£400.13	£1,100.13
10	£75.00	£115.20	£775.00	£515.33	£1,290.33
11	£75.00	£135.11	£850.00	£650.45	£1,500.45
12	£75.00	£157.12	£925.00	£807.56	£1,732.56
13	£75.00	£181.42	£1,000.00	£988.99	£1,988.99
14	£75.00	£208.27	£1,075.00	£1,197.26	£2,272.26
15	£75.00	£237.94	£1,150.00	£1,435.19	£2,585.19
16	£75.00	£270.70	£1,225.00	£1,705.90	£2,930.90
17	£75.00	£306.90	£1,300.00	£2,012.80	£3,312.80
18	£75.00	£346.89	£1,375.00	£2,359.69	£3,734.69
19	£75.00	£391.07	£1,450.00	£2,750.77	£4,200.77
20	£75.00	£439.88	£1,525.00	£3,190.64	£4,715.64
21	£75.00	£493.79	£1,600.00	£3,684.43	£5,284.43
22	£75.00	£553.35	£1,675.00	£4,237.78	£5,912.78
23	£75.00	£619.15	£1,750.00	£4,856.92	£6,606.92
24	£75.00	£691.83	£1,825.00	£5,548.75	£7,373.75
25	£75.00	£772.13	£1,900.00	£6,320.88	£8,220.88

Additional contributions applied at the end of each period, following interest calculation.

This is the power of compound interest and investing as early as you possibly can.

It's still the same £1,900 that you have physically handed over, invested over the same twenty-five years. Look at the orange column. That is the earned interest projections. You can see it is just £2.62 in year one, but by year twenty-five that investment pot has earned £6,320.88 cumulatively in interest based on a 10% a year return.

That orange column is why rich people get richer and poor people stay poor. It is because rich people understand that you can start small and let the money do the work. Yes, there is risk attached because you are investing but remember that some of the lowest risk investments available, like the S&P 500 or the FTSE 100, on average return 10% per annum.

S&P 500 Historical Annual Returns

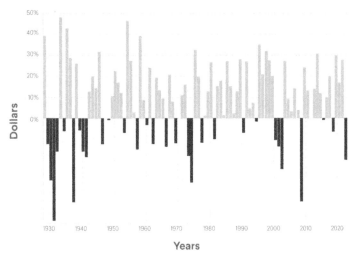

This really helpful diagram taken from an article by Rebecca Lake, on SoFi, shows the ups and downs of the S&P 500 since 1930 (https://www.sofi.com/learn/content/average-stock-market-return/ the full article is here). You will see that actually there isn't really an average of 10% a year. It is either much higher or much lower than 10%. But when we are looking over time and remembering that we are working on this as a long-term plan, you can take the average over time. When you look at the long-term average, it is around 10% per year.

Here are some more example scenarios of how you could put compound interest to work to create financial freedom for the next generation if you start from the day they are born.

This scenario is how you can create a pot worth £1,000,000 on someone's thirty-fifth birthday.

I don't know about you, but if my parents had handed me a pot worth £1,000,000 on my thirty-fifth birthday, life would look very different for me right now. These are the sorts of things that happen in wealthy households all the time but don't happen in our world because our parents weren't taught this, their parents weren't taught this and we haven't been taught this. So, here goes.

If you take £1,000 as your starting pot. I know this is a tough milestone to reach. Hopefully, with what we have discussed around debt and money management, getting to this milestone will be easier for you.

£1,000 invested into the FTSE 100 or S&P 500 on day one at **10% per year.**

Add in **£254.80** per month for thirty-five years.

You will have invested a total of **£108,016** of your own capital into the pot.

You will have earned **£892,006.03** in interest from your 10% per year.

It will be worth (as long as you never withdraw from it) **£1,000,022.03** on that child's thirty-fifth birthday.

MONEY MECHANICS

Year	Deposits & Withdrawals	Interest	Total Deposits & Withdrawals	Accrued Interest	Balance
0	£1,000.00	–	£1,000.00	–	£1,000.00
1	£3,057.60	£248.82	£4,057.60	£248.82	£4,306.42
2	£3,057.60	£595.05	£7,115.20	£843.86	£7,959.06
3	£3,057.60	£977.52	£10,172.80	£1,821.39	£11,994.19
4	£3,057.60	£1,400.06	£13,230.40	£3,221.45	£16,451.85
5	£3,057.60	£1,866.83	£16,288.00	£5,088.27	£21,376.27
6	£3,057.60	£2,382.48	£19,345.60	£7,470.76	£26,816.36
7	£3,057.60	£2,952.13	£22,403.20	£10,422.89	£32,826.09
8	£3,057.60	£3,581.43	£25,460.80	£14,004.31	£39,465.11
9	£3,057.60	£4,276.62	£28,518.40	£18,280.93	£46,799.33
10	£3,057.60	£5,044.61	£31,576.00	£23,325.54	£54,901.54
11	£3,057.60	£5,893.02	£34,633.60	£29,218.56	£63,852.16
12	£3,057.60	£6,830.26	£37,691.20	£36,048.82	£73,740.02
13	£3,057.60	£7,865.65	£40,748.80	£43,914.47	£84,663.27
14	£3,057.60	£9,009.46	£43,806.40	£52,923.93	£96,730.33
15	£3,057.60	£10,273.04	£46,864.00	£63,196.96	£110,060.96
16	£3,057.60	£11,668.93	£49,921.60	£74,865.89	£124,787.49
17	£3,057.60	£13,210.99	£52,979.20	£88,076.88	£141,056.08
18	£3,057.60	£14,914.52	£56,036.80	£102,991.40	£159,028.20
19	£3,057.60	£16,796.44	£59,094.40	£119,787.84	£178,882.24
20	£3,057.60	£18,875.41	£62,152.00	£138,663.25	£200,815.25
21	£3,057.60	£21,172.09	£65,209.60	£159,835.34	£225,044.94
22	£3,057.60	£23,709.25	£68,267.20	£183,544.59	£251,811.79
23	£3,057.60	£26,512.09	£71,324.80	£210,056.69	£281,381.49
24	£3,057.60	£29,608.43	£74,382.40	£239,665.11	£314,047.51
25	£3,057.60	£33,028.98	£77,440.00	£272,694.10	£350,134.10
26	£3,057.60	£36,807.72	£80,497.60	£309,501.82	£389,999.42
27	£3,057.60	£40,982.14	£83,555.20	£350,483.96	£434,039.16
28	£3,057.60	£45,593.68	£86,612.80	£396,077.64	£482,690.44
29	£3,057.60	£50,688.10	£89,670.40	£446,765.74	£536,436.14
30	£3,057.60	£56,315.98	£92,728.00	£503,081.72	£595,809.72
31	£3,057.60	£62,533.17	£95,785.60	£565,614.89	£661,400.49
32	£3,057.60	£69,401.38	£98,843.20	£635,016.27	£733,859.47
33	£3,057.60	£76,988.78	£101,900.80	£712,005.06	£813,905.86
34	£3,057.60	£85,370.69	£104,958.40	£797,375.74	£902,334.14
35	£3,057.60	£94,630.28	£108,016.00	£892,006.03	£1,000,022.03

Additional contributions applied at the end of each period, following interest calculation.

But what if you are in your forties already and only just learning about this stuff?

What would have to happen for you to be able to reach fifty-five with a pot worth £500,000?

It is possible but sadly, time isn't on your side so you will have to contribute more to begin with. The numbers look like this if you stick to a low risk 10% per annum.

To build a pot worth £500,000 in fifteen years, you would need to do the following:

£10,000 invested into the FTSE 100 or S&P 500 (other funds are available) on day one at **10% per year.**

Add in **£1,099** per month for fifteen years.

You will have invested a total of **£207,820** of your own capital into the pot.

You will have earned **£292.222.11** in interest from your 10% per year.

It will be worth (as long as you never withdraw from it) **£500,042.11.**

Year	Deposits & Withdrawals	Interest	Total Deposits & Withdrawals	Accrued Interest	Balance
0	£10,000.00	–	£10,000.00	–	£10,000.00
1	£13,188.00	£1,668.69	£23,188.00	£1,668.69	£24,856.69
2	£13,188.00	£3,224.38	£36,376.00	£4,893.07	£41,269.07
3	£13,188.00	£4,942.97	£49,564.00	£9,836.04	£59,400.04
4	£13,188.00	£6,841.52	£62,752.00	£16,677.56	£79,429.56
5	£13,188.00	£8,938.87	£75,940.00	£25,616.43	£101,556.43
6	£13,188.00	£11,255.84	£89,128.00	£36,872.28	£126,000.28
7	£13,188.00	£13,815.43	£102,316.00	£50,687.71	£153,003.71
8	£13,188.00	£16,643.05	£115,504.00	£67,330.76	£182,834.76
9	£13,188.00	£19,766.75	£128,692.00	£87,097.51	£215,789.51
10	£13,188.00	£23,217.54	£141,880.00	£110,315.05	£252,195.05
11	£13,188.00	£27,029.68	£155,068.00	£137,344.72	£292,412.72
12	£13,188.00	£31,240.99	£168,256.00	£168,585.72	£336,841.72
13	£13,188.00	£35,893.29	£181,444.00	£204,479.00	£385,923.00
14	£13,188.00	£41,032.74	£194,632.00	£245,511.75	£440,143.75
15	£13,188.00	£46,710.36	£207,820.00	£292,222.11	£500,042.11

Additional contributions applied at the end of each period, following interest calculation.

Now, I can hear many of you thinking "I don't have £1,099 a month to invest", and I get it, that is a big chunk of change for most people. The thing about investing is that if you have a target outcome then you can tweak the numbers. If you have less capital then it is likely you may need to look at finding a higher return or waiting for more years to hit your goal.

Let's look at a higher return scenario, which would come with much higher risk levels.

This time we start with an initial investment of £50 and you invest it into a much higher-risk opportunity that can provide a 2.62% return a month.

Actively managed Forex funds and Crypto funds can achieve these results but in a risky way. I will dig more into that in the chapter on these topics. I have funds invested into a Forex fund that returns 15% a month right now, but this is a bit more like gambling than it is investing. The reason I tell you is that I want you to understand that these opportunities are out there. You need to find the right opportunities for you, do your due diligence and make sure you diversify.

Remember, **NEVER INVEST WHAT YOU CAN'T AFFORD TO LOSE** and diversify, diversify, diversify.

£50 invested into a high-risk fund paying 2.62% a month

Add in £125 per month for fifteen years

You will have invested a total of £22,550 of your own capital into the pot

You will have earned £479,551.01 in interest from your 2.62% per month

It will be worth (as long as you never withdraw from it and it maintains a consistent 2.62%) **£502,101.01 after fifteen years.**

Year	Deposits & Withdrawals	Interest	Total Deposits & Withdrawals	Accrued Interest	Balance
0	£50.00	–	£50.00	–	£50.00
1	£1,500.00	£254.38	£1,550.00	£254.38	£1,804.38
2	£1,500.00	£892.81	£3,050.00	£1,147.20	£4,197.20
3	£1,500.00	£1,763.57	£4,550.00	£2,910.76	£7,460.76
4	£1,500.00	£2,951.20	£6,050.00	£5,861.96	£11,911.96
5	£1,500.00	£4,571.01	£7,550.00	£10,432.97	£17,982.97
6	£1,500.00	£6,780.28	£9,050.00	£17,213.25	£26,263.25
7	£1,500.00	£9,793.52	£10,550.00	£27,006.77	£37,556.77
8	£1,500.00	£13,903.28	£12,050.00	£40,910.05	£52,960.05
9	£1,500.00	£19,508.62	£13,550.00	£60,418.67	£73,968.67
10	£1,500.00	£27,153.76	£15,050.00	£87,572.43	£102,622.43
11	£1,500.00	£37,581.00	£16,550.00	£125,153.43	£141,703.43
12	£1,500.00	£51,802.78	£18,050.00	£176,956.21	£195,006.21
13	£1,500.00	£71,199.92	£19,550.00	£248,156.14	£267,706.14
14	£1,500.00	£97,655.79	£21,050.00	£345,811.93	£366,861.93
15	£1,500.00	£133,739.08	£22,550.00	£479,551.01	£502,101.01

Additional contributions applied at the end of each period, following interest calculation.

Now, I want to reiterate that 2.62% a month is a really high return. It is risky and is not something that a lot of people can actually maintain with no losses, so you must do your research and make sure you are keeping an eye on it, tracking performance regularly and ensuring that your funds are hitting the goals you set out to achieve. I am not advising you to play a risky game. I want to offer you a scenario so you can get to grips with how you could approach your financial targets. Take a look at the compound interest calculator on my website. Put your numbers in and it will show you exactly what returns you need, over how many years, and what you need to contribute financially in order to reach your targets. www.sarahpoynton.com/moneymechanicsresources

What I hope you will take away from this section of the book is that investing and using compound interest is achievable for you regardless of where you're starting. If you have £10 or £1,000 to start, if you have £10 a month or £1,000 a month to contribute to it, the point is that you can start now. Make use of compound interest so your money grows. This just doesn't happen when you leave your money static in a bank savings account, being eroded by inflation every day.

Making use of compound interest will see you achieve financial independence faster than you ever thought possible. You can make your children financially independent (if you choose to have them), and you can be a wealthy, financially secure and abundant person that only ever makes decisions from a place of choice.

Imagine the example we can set for future generations - sons, daughters, nieces and nephews, and our friends. Imagine a life where everything you do is because you choose it! That is the name of the game for me. Actual choice through financial independence.

A really useful resource you can use to play around with these numbers is the compound interest calculator on my website www.sarahpoynton.com/moneymechanicsresources.

Determine your goals and use this calculator to help you see exactly what you need to do to create your wealth using compound interest.

Happy number crunching.

CHAPTER 9

BEYOND THE BALANCE: LEVERAGING CREDIT REWARDS FOR MORE MILEAGE

This chapter is going to be really fun.

Have you ever looked online at Instagram or social media in general and seen people flying first class or eating in the best restaurants and thought to yourself "I wish I could fly first class" or wondered how they manage to travel so much and where do they get their money from to afford these crazy expensive seats?

Well, this chapter will tell you how you can live a luxurious life even if your income has a ceiling right now because let me tell you something, most of the people you see sitting in first class have not paid the full ticket price for those seats. Another thing the wealthy world doesn't do a very good job of sharing is that people with money don't pay full price for most things. Not only do they negotiate on everything - and I mean everything - but they also use rewards and points and clever Money Mechanics to make every pound go further.

Let me tell you about my first ever first-class flight. There is something pretty special about getting on a plane and turning left. Now, for the super-wealthy, this is just standard practice, it is what they come to expect but for me, getting on a plane and turning left was something I had always wanted to do but figured, because I wasn't a gazillionaire, that wouldn't happen for me. I don't know if you have ever even looked at the first-class option for a long-haul flight but we are talking thousands and thousands if you just book it paying the standard ticket price. In my mind, I could never really justify four months' mortgage payments on being able to lie down for eleven hours.

Then I discovered that no one (with any sense) pays full price for those seats and that most people you see in First and Business on planes are there on some kind of rewards package that has allowed them to upgrade or pay for flights without needing money. What an absolute game-changer.

The first time I flew first class, I entered a world of travel that is honestly the best thing ever - being greeted by name, being offered silk pyjamas and champagne on arrival, real cutlery, a bed with a pillow and a good night's sleep. If you have ever tried to convince yourself that it's just not worth flying first class then I hate to break it to you, but it really is... But only if you don't take on debt or break the bank to do it.

The first time I flew first class, I went from London to LA and back again and it cost me a total of £350, around $435. I flew with British Airways and it was probably the most fun £350 I have ever spent. What an experience!

The seat I had, if I had booked it online and paid the ticket price for it would have been £8,000 roughly ($9,946). I don't know about you, but even with my financial situation now, almost 10k for a bit of comfort for twelve hours feels like a stretch when my husband and I managed to travel around the world for three months in 2016 for under £10k. But I do love the experience of that comfort and I want that in my life, so I engineer things so that I build up rewards and points which means I can pay £350 airport tax and get my flights paid for by the rewards.

The first one I am going to tell you about is American Express. Not all retailers/suppliers take this card but many of them do. In the US, more people are geared up to take AMEX but in the UK and Europe, there is sometimes the challenge of "we don't take Amex", which is annoying. Putting that to one side, having an Amex card is going to change your life, remember it isn't about how much money you can make, it is all about how you engineer that money to maximise its value.

I have a British Airways Avios Points American Express and I have an American Express Gold Card. There are loads of other options though based on your spending habits etc. I started with the "Blue One", as I lovingly call it. It is the British Airways American Express Credit Card. It is a personal card, not a business card, so it's available to you whether you have a business or not.

There are business options available too.

The link for you to apply for your own is below. This is a referral link and, for full transparency, when you are approved and use it in your first three months, you will get a joining reward of 10,000 free Avios points and Amex drop me 4000 points for recommending to you as well! We both win!

https://americanexpress.com/en-gb/referral/sARAHPjGMz? CPID=100402650

First, let me tell you what these points mean and then how you can leverage them to fly first class to LA (other destinations are available of course). As I spend money on things, I get points back from Avios and those Avios points are all stored in my account until I want to use them. I can use them for flights, hotels, car hire, baggage allowance increase, upgrades, experiences, airport lounges and more. There are a number of airlines that take part in the Avios program. I have a British Airways card but I can fly using the points on any of the involved airlines, which gives you lots of flexibility when trying to choose flights.

This week, I was looking at birthday trip flights for my big 4-0 coming up and Business Class flights for my husband and I to fly from London to the Bahamas in mid-July are under £400 each using just my points.

Each Avios point is worth between 0.38p and 2.1p, depending on which type of seat you book. The higher your cabin class, the more valuable your Avios points become. It takes longer to earn more points but when you redeem them they are worth more.

For example, as of today while writing this, a return flight from London Gatwick to Bangkok in Economy would be 83,000 points plus £315.67 in taxes. So if you have 83,000 points, you could pay £315.67 and fly there and back.

The same flights in first class would be 250,000 Avios points plus £546.31. So you pay the £546.31 and use your points and you fly first class there and back.

And to take this one layer further. Amex runs a program called the companion voucher, so when you have spent £12,000 on your card, you get automatically given a voucher and that means that whatever flight you are booking, you get a matching seat free for someone to join you. So you can book two seats for the price of one.

Those tickets will include a meet and greet at check-in, a giant 90kg weight allowance in many cases, first boarding, champagne on entry to the plane, incredible food and drink the whole way, a private cabin, the most incredible cabin crew who have all the time in the world to look after you because they only have eight people to look after for twelve hours instead of 500 people between a few of them. And the kicker - if you use rewards, you have probably paid less to have that experience than most of the people sitting at the back.

When I first started to become aware of these things I was grumpy that I hadn't discovered this sooner. I was also excited that I could get involved. I always thought that only the really rich had American Express cards. I only applied for it because someone I was working with told me that I should. I had debt and I didn't have a good credit score - it wasn't the worst it had ever been but it wasn't great. I thought there was no way I would ever get approved for a 'rich person's' credit card, but I did and you might too!

Once you have it, there are some important rules though.

Remember we talked about the B.A.A.T system in the debt chapter?

Avoiding new debt is step two of this system. If you are going to take out an Amex (or any credit card for rewards) then you must follow this rule, otherwise, it doesn't make you financially stronger, it will make you financially weaker.

YOU MUST PAY OFF THE FULL BALANCE, EVERY SINGLE MONTH, WITHOUT FAIL!

This is non-negotiable.

Not sometimes.

Not when you have enough money.

You **MUST** clear it in full every month or this doesn't work.

So, start small. If you drive, you will be paying for petrol every week. Instead of paying on your debit card at the station, pay on your Amex and then, that same day, transfer the exact amount that you spent from the debit card you would have used straight onto your Amex. You have still spent the same £100 to fill up your car but by engineering things differently, you have been given 100 points that you can use to pay for things elsewhere. FREE MONEY! Then, once you start getting used to it, you can start to pay for more things.

Now I pay for everything I possibly can on my Amex. Subscriptions to things, food, petrol, dinners, drinks, travel, trains, flights, the tube, clothes, bills, DIY, and anything I order on Amazon. It soon adds up.

If you bank with Barclays Premier, for example, you can upgrade your account for £12 a month and you will receive 18,000 Avios points as a bonus per year. If you aren't a Barclays customer (I am not) but you want to be and switch, they will give you the 18,000 points per year plus a switching bonus of 25,000 points. More free money!

Imagine if you are planning and paying for a wedding. The average wedding, according to research, costs around £24,000. And then you have the honeymoon on top, an average of around £4,000. Well, if you were to pay for your whole wedding on an Amex card and earn Avios points, you could use those points to pay for your flights and hotel for your honeymoon. How do free flights on your Honeymoon sound?

You see, this is where money can be made to go so much further. If, for every pound you spend, you get back some sort of reward point or cashback that can then be used for something else, then you are making your money go so much further.

I obviously can't tell you to go and get a credit card, this is a personal choice. I have never once regretted having an Amex because my money simply goes further. Of course, other rewards credit cards are available and you must find the right one for you. Now you know the power of using rewards like this, you can go and discover what the right options for you are.

If you are not ready for a credit card yet, there are still lots of ways to get your hands on free luxury swag through rewards and points systems that are everywhere when you really start to look.

Let's start with something as simple as Amazon Prime. It blows my mind that some people still don't have this rewards program.

Most people think this is just a "free shipping" subscription. That in itself makes it worth it in my opinion but it is so much more than that. £95 a year or £8.99 a month and for that you get:

- Unlimited one-day delivery on millions of items on Amazon (that you can pay for on an Amex or rewards payment card)
- Prime Now if same-day delivery isn't fast enough this gives you around 25,000 items to your door within two hours
- Prime Video which is quickly becoming a real competitive player in the movie streaming space
- Unlimited music streaming with Prime Music
- Amazon music unlimited
- Unlimited photo storage
- Amazing reading benefits for those of you that read with Kindle Lending Library, Prime Reading and Kindle First included in your Prime membership
- New Audible listening channels
- Big discounts on video games

- Premium Twitch.tv features
- Prime Pantry will deliver groceries and household goods straight to your door (in some parts of the world)
- Discount on premium channels such as Showtime & Starz
- Wickedly prime which is the delivery of snacks

The list of things included in Prime membership is vast and very underutilised by most people.

Rewards and loyalty programs are everywhere.

BP gives you two points for every one litre of Ultimate fuel or one point for every one litre of regular fuel, and for every £1 you spend in-store, you get one point. So, if the average car takes between 45 and 65 litres of fuel and let's say you fill up twice a month, that is 1080 to 1560 points a year just for buying things that you would be buying anyway.

Now, this is where this becomes super sexy. BP will now allow you to convert to Avios points so if you use your Amex to pay for fuel and get a BP Loyalty card, you get the points for every pound spent on Amex and a point for every litre on your BP card and then you can turn them into Avios points, so you get points on the same money spent, twice. Amazing, right?

If you don't want Avios you can redeem these vouchers at hundreds of other retailers and you can use these vouchers to buy other things that you need.

Iceland gives you £1 back on every £20 you spend in-store.

Tesco gives you one point for every £1 you spend in-store.

A Nectar card gives you one point for every £1 spent in Argos and Sainsburys.

At Starbucks, they give you stars. Collect150 Stars and you get a free drink. 450 stars you reach GOLD status and GOLD members get free extras, like cream and syrups, on the house.

There was a period of my life where I never got these cards and I didn't bother with them because I thought, what difference does a few points really make? But when added up across every single thing you buy every single month, it makes a huge difference.

I have an account with an app called Crypto.com. This is a cryptocurrency app and I am not here to tell you that you should or shouldn't invest in crypto but what I am going to tell you is how I get 100% cash back on my Netflix and Spotify subscriptions every month. Sound good?

I set up my account using this link https://crypto.com/app/c6zhusnamx. They will give you $25 free crypto as a joining bonus if you decide to join. You can use that in the app to make your first crypto investment. That is risk-free because it was free money to begin with. We talk more about this in the crypto and forex chapter later.

What I want to tell you about here is 100% cashback on Netflix and Spotify.

When I joined, I applied for a Crypto.com VISA card. This is simply a debit card that can be used in all shops just like your bank Visa card. The difference between this card and my other Visa cards is that when I pay for my Netflix and Spotify subscriptions using this card, I get 100% of the subscription back in cryptocurrency credited to my account every month.

I also get free airport lounge passes with a guest, 8% CRO lockup rewards and other interest-based bonuses which result in the value of my money going up. I spend £15.99 on Netflix but I get it all back. I imagine most people reading this are subscribed to

Netflix but I bet you don't get 100% cashback on your £15.99 a month. If you are, great work, if you are not, then you can!

If you are paying for it then that money is spent anyway - it is a liability, it is draining your resources. When I spend £15.99 a month, I get back 8.2082 CRO every month. The exciting thing about that is that I own the currency and the value of that currency goes up and down with the market. Because it is a monthly transaction, I am using dollar cost averaging to acquire digital currency for free. I get the same 100% cash back on my Spotify subscription as well. Cool, huh?

It doesn't seem like a lot, does it? £15 here, £9.99 there. But when you bring everything together, what you actually can do is have most of your liabilities paid for by someone or something else.

Now, to be eligible for this level of reward, I had to apply for the Royal Indigo or Jade Green visa card. To be eligible for this card and these rewards, I had to stake £3,000 into my account. If that isn't possible for you right away, there is a lower level that allows you to stake £300 and you still get your Spotify fully refunded with CRO currency every month.

Anywhere that doesn't take Amex, I will tend to use my crypto.com card because I won't get Amex points but I do get 2% cash back in crypto on everything I spend. I get £15.99 a month in crypto for my Netflix subscription and £9.99 a month in crypto for my Spotify account. That is £311.76 a year, plus the cashback, that I am being paid for using that card and because that is automatically being put in my account as CRO, it means I am investing £311.76 into crypto every year and I am not doing anything other than paying for my Netflix and Spotify, which most people are doing every month anyway.

If you bring into play compound interest over five years of subscriptions, and assume the CRO will return a minimum of 5% a year (which is highly possible), then inside of five years, that refund on your Netflix and Spotify subscriptions, that you would be paying for anyway, is a pot of money worth £21,601. That is free money, just by paying for things a little bit differently than you are now. You aren't having to cut out the things you are using to increase your wealth, you are just using Money Mechanics tactics to make your money work harder for you.

We have talked about the luxurious end of this with travel and champagne, we have talked about the much more unknown world of crypto cashback and rewards and the very simple free whipped cream from Starbucks. What I hope you will take away from this chapter is that putting your money to work doesn't just mean investing it and risking it. When you engineer your money using rewards and points and loyalty programs, you will live a far less expensive life but still have all the things you are buying now and possibly more.

Living an abundant life doesn't happen by cutting out everything. That is no life at all! Life is about living. Living an abundant life is available when you engineer your money and make it go further!

It is always great when you can have your cake and eat it too - especially when the cake is free!

CHAPTER 10

THE FUCK YOU MONEY FUND: YOUR PATH TO UNCOMPROMISED FREEDOM

This is going to be the shortest chapter of this book but probably one of the most important. In this chapter, I am going to give you the exact Money Mechanics formula that will give you the lifestyle you want without ever having to go to work and trade your time for money again.

Believe it or not, there is a mathematical formula that anyone can use and it gives you the answer to "how much money is enough money" for you personally.

Most of us strive our whole lives to find a way to maintain the lifestyle we want without taking a hit on our income.

If you want to go travelling for six months, most people have to quit their jobs. If you want to spend two months volunteering in Bali in an elephant sanctuary without any wifi or signal, most people would lose their income. Most people work their whole lives to get to retirement, when they finally have time to themselves, but then they have to live on a measly pension unless they have engineered their money well throughout their life.

Let's say you retire at sixty-five and live until you are ninety-five and are used to an income of £30,000 a year at the point you retire. For you to maintain the same lifestyle you have had up until the point you retire, you need to have £900,000 in the bank.

Let's say you want to retire at sixty and you are used to an income of £50,000 at the point you retired. If you lived to ninety, you would need £1,500,000 in the bank at the point you retire to sustain that £50,000 a year lifestyle after you retire.

What if you retire at sixty and live to ninety-five with a £30,000 a year life? You need £1,050,000 in the bank.

Retire at sixty and live to ninety-five with a £50,000 life? You need £1,750,000 in the bank.

As an aside, I don't know about you, but I actually don't know many people who have ever actually done this calculation and worked out what they need in the bank to maintain their lifestyle at the point they retire. And retirement can come at any age by the way. That is actually something you can choose. Just because society tells us that you have to work until you are sixty-five doesn't actually mean you have to. There is a whole movement in our generation called FIRE, Financially Independent Retired Early. Basically, people who put the work into becoming financially independent first and then living financially free for as much of their life as they can.

Now, a little reality check here. If you have earned £30,000 a year your whole life you would have paid tax on that so you actually likely took home around £24,000 a year. If you earned that from the day you started working at eighteen to the day you retired at sixty-five, then you have earned a total of £1,128,000 in your working life. And you had to live and eat and pay bills and raise humans and pay for holidays. All the things!

It is IMPOSSIBLE for you to save £1,050,000 ready for retirement when you have only actually earned £1,128,000 in your whole working life. And let's be real, most of you are not going to earn £30,000 from the day you turn 18 for your whole life. The only way you can prepare for life after work without taking the hit on your financial position is to invest.

There simply is no other way. Even winning the lottery is unlikely to work because first of all, you have to hope you win and hope is not a strategy, but secondly, most people who have a huge influx of wealth very quickly tend to lose it just as fast because they have not learned to be a Money Mechanic.

Who do you know that is approaching retirement age that is just never going to be able to retire without also giving up the lifestyle they have because they just don't have the income lined up? I bet you know a load of people like this. I know I do.

We have talked throughout this book about how money in the bank is dead money. Because of the joys of inflation, when you have money sitting in the bank, it is eroding every day. It is, quite literally, the worst place to keep your cash. Well, under the mattress is the worst place, the bank is the next worst! Inflation is eroding the buying power of your money when it is in a savings account if inflation is higher than the interest rate you are getting.

You are a Money Mechanic now. Instead of letting your money devalue over time, you are going to put it to work so it increases in value instead. You have to have a target to have a big enough portfolio of investments that it pays you your annual wages without you ever having to trade time for money again.

This is what I (and a few other people) call the **Fuck You Money Fund!**

The term Fuck You Money has been floating around since Burt Reynolds said it in the movie Heat in the 80s. John Goodman has a short monologue in the movie The Gambler that explains the concept really well. You can watch the clip over on my website if you fancy it www.sarahpoynton.com/moneymechanicsresources

The concept of 'Fuck You Money' is when you have enough wealth or financial independence to be able to walk away from a job or situation without ever having to worry about the consequences that decision will have on you or your family financially. It is the amount of money you need to be able to say "fuck you" to any situation that is no longer serving you or bringing you joy.

Having 'fuck you' money brings the power back to you. It gives you a platform to take risks without the constraints of money holding you back. It gives you a life that is on your terms, where you can pursue your passions, work on projects, write books, make things and visit places, despite those things being a labour of love and not necessarily giving you an income. It gives you the opportunity to leave a violent or toxic relationship, walk away from a job that is making you ill, or start a business that you always considered but were too time-poor to give a real go. It gives you the freedom to take a year off to travel, volunteer, spend time with family or care for a loved one.

"Fuck You Money" is a different figure for everyone, but we all have a "Fuck You Money" number and I am going to tell you how to work out yours.

Are you ready?

The formula is here:

Annual Target Income (what you want to earn per year)

Multiplied by twenty-five

Invested at 4% per annum

= Fuck You Money

(this is the simple formula and does not adjust for inflation)

If you want the digital version of this, you can go to my website and use the calculator to get your fuck you money number www.sarahpoynton.com/moneymechanicsresources

I use 4% in this format because many banks' savings pay higher than 4% interest. There are LOTS of places you can achieve 4% on your money. This is low risk and will work with most people's risk profiles.

If you currently earn £50,000 a year and you want to maintain your lifestyle but be able to say "Fuck You" to your job, then you need to work towards a pot of £1,250,000 and have it invested at 4% per annum, then you can walk away.

If you take this one step further and consider your risk profile, you might be someone that is happier with a slightly higher risk. Looking at something like the S&P 500, which averages 10% per year, then you actually only need £500,000 invested at 10% to create the same £50,000 a year. Obviously, you wouldn't put everything you have in one place, remember to diversify, but this demonstrates the options.

If you are someone that wants to go higher-risk, then you can find other ways to build a portfolio that achieves 20% a year, which would mean you need a pot of £250,000 invested at an average of 20% per year to create your £50,000 a year income.

Now, I know that building a pot of £250,000 is a tall order for most people in a short space of time and that is why Money

Mechanics like you start early and invest with the long game in mind. We make use of the power of compounding interest over time. When you do this, that pot of £250,000 is possible in a much shorter time frame.

In fact, if you took £1,000 on your eighteenth Birthday and added £250 a month to it in an investment vehicle such as the S&P 500, achieving an average of 10% per year, then you would have your £500,000 on your forty-eighth birthday, so you could retire on £50,000 a year at forty-eight and not have to reduce your lifestyle in any way - if you wanted to.

Retiring at forty-eight sounds better than sixty-five, doesn't it?

Let me show you how you can help your children retire at forty on £50,000 a year if they wanted to.

£2,000 on their eighteenth birthday, invested into a mix of assets generating an average of 15.2% per annum, with £250 a month added to it, left to compound for twenty-two years is £505,820. So on their fortieth birthday, they have a £50,000 a year "Fuck You Money" fund.

But what if you are in your fifties or sixties and trying to get into an FYM position? Well, you don't have as much time on your hands, but getting started sooner rather than later is the first thing. You could work with a mix of risk profiles and use the income from your higher-risk investments to be contributing more each month to your FYM pot.

The initial capital of £2,000 on your 50th birthday, adding £500 a month until you are sixty-two, invested at 20% per annum (which will likely be a higher risk), gives you an FYM pot of £277,000 in twelve years.

Most people spend their whole life trying to figure out when enough will be enough. Well, your FYM number is the answer to that question.

If you want an income of £150,000 a year, you need an FYM fund of £3,750,000 invested at 4% per year.

If you want an income of £100,000 a year, you need an FYM fund of £2,500,000 invested at 4% per year.

Now you know how to work this out for yourself, there is no excuse. Get the number in your brain, and then you can start doing everything you can to be adding to it all the time.

I know people that have built a £250,000 FYM fund in twelve months. It is £684.94 a day. They have sold things, mowed lawns for people, cleared rubbish for people, been an Uber Eats driver on the side of their job and used platforms like Vinted to sell things they don't want anymore for a few pounds instead of just giving things away to the charity shop. They have acted as affiliates for existing companies and have been paid a commission. They have helped solve problems for people and been paid for the work and put everything they have earned straight into their FYM fund. It is bloody hard work but it is possible and it is possible for you if you mean it when you say you want Fuck You Money.

Are you willing to do whatever it takes to work on your Fuck You Money Fund?

My top tip for this is that unless you work out the number and get laser-focused on it, you will never hit it. Make it visible, look at it daily, stay the distance, trust the process and do the work!

You are a Money Mechanic now! You Got This!

Below is the Fuck You Money Matrix. You will be able to find the annual figure you are looking to achieve and you can work out what amount you need to build up in your pot and at what percentage in order to be able to say you have Fuck You Money.

It is small here in the book so you can get a bigger copy of this from my website

www.sarahpoynton.com/moneymechanicsresources

Annual Income Target	4%	5%	6%	7%	8%	9%	10%	11%	12%	13%	14%	15%	16%	17%	18%	19%	20%
25,000	625,000	500,000	416,667	357,143	312,500	277,778	250,000	227,273	208,333	192,308	178,571	166,667	156,250	147,059	138,889	131,579	125,000
50,000	1,250,000	1,000,000	833,333	714,286	625,000	555,556	500,000	454,545	416,667	384,615	357,143	333,333	312,500	294,118	277,778	263,158	250,000
75,000	1,875,000	1,500,000	1,250,000	1,071,429	937,500	833,333	750,000	681,818	625,000	576,923	535,714	500,000	468,750	441,176	416,667	394,737	375,000
100,000	2,500,000	2,000,000	1,666,667	1,428,571	1,250,000	1,111,111	1,000,000	909,091	833,333	769,231	714,286	666,667	625,000	588,235	555,556	526,316	500,000
125,000	3,125,000	2,500,000	2,083,333	1,785,714	1,562,500	1,388,889	1,250,000	1,136,364	1,041,667	961,538	892,857	833,333	781,250	735,294	694,444	657,895	625,000
150,000	3,750,000	3,000,000	2,500,000	2,142,857	1,875,000	1,666,667	1,500,000	1,363,636	1,250,000	1,153,846	1,071,429	1,000,000	937,500	882,353	833,333	789,474	750,000
175,000	4,375,000	3,500,000	2,916,667	2,500,000	2,187,500	1,944,444	1,750,000	1,590,909	1,458,333	1,346,154	1,250,000	1,166,667	1,093,750	1,029,412	972,222	921,053	875,000
200,000	5,000,000	4,000,000	3,333,333	2,857,143	2,500,000	2,222,222	2,000,000	1,818,182	1,666,667	1,538,462	1,428,571	1,333,333	1,250,000	1,176,471	1,111,111	1,052,632	1,000,000

The Fuck You Money Matrix

CHAPTER 11

DARE TO DARE: UNDERSTANDING AND MITIGATING INVESTMENT UNCERTAINTY

There is always a ying to the yang, a love to the hate, a dark to the light.

As Money Mechanics, we must be clued up on what risk comes into play as we work on our financial independence. You must understand how to assess your risk profile and some of the ways you can mitigate risk so that you are never in a situation where you lose all the money you have worked really hard to build up.

I want you to understand though that at some point you will lose some money. That is the nature of the beast I am afraid. That is investing. But when you understand risk and you implement tactics to mitigate and control the risk, then you will still grow wealth despite the odd loss.

Risk comes with the territory. You might make a bad decision or allow your emotions to get in the way. You might panic sell or maybe you invest in a business that is run poorly and goes bust, making your investment worth zero.

At some stage, it is going to happen. That is the very honest truth. Risk is something you cannot escape, you cannot control it but you can plan for it, mitigate it and choose to deal with it.

Risk refers to the likelihood of losing money or not achieving the expected return on investment you had hoped for.

People often say "Investing in the markets is too risky" or buying stocks and shares "is just like going to Vegas and putting it all on black". Yes, there is a degree of uncertainty or chance associated with investing but unlike sticking everything on the spin of a roulette wheel, where the outcome is entirely random, the risks associated with investing can be analysed, diversified against and managed.

As a Money Mechanic, you have a few things you must consider before making investment decisions. Market risk is the most common. This is the risk that the value of your investment will fluctuate due to changes in the market - changes such as political decisions or natural disasters. It is a bit like a roller coaster, a little unpredictable. But just like a roller coaster, a Money Mechanic understands that they have to ride the whole ride to get their feet back on solid ground.

The key to managing risk is diversification.

This means spreading your available funds across a number of different asset classes, sectors, and regions. Diversification sets you up with some protections so that if one fails, the others can make up for the loss. Diversification is the key. You must diversify your investments to increase the chances of achieving your investment goals.

How do you actually diversify though?

If you think about a well-balanced diet, when you consume different types of food the body receives different nutrients from those different things, right?

That is what we are doing when we diversify our portfolios. We are feeding our financial independence from lots of smaller channels, instead of putting all our eggs in one basket, so to speak.

That is why this book isn't a book that just talks about property or stocks or funds. It is a book that talks about all of the different tools that you can mix together to create financial independence as a Money Mechanic. It is the foundation of diversification to know and use multiple routes to wealth.

Putting all of your money into one place creates a single point of failure and that is such a risky strategy. In his book "Reminiscences of a Stock Operator", Edwin Lefevre, a respected American Journalist and Wall Street Stock Broker, shared his story of how he invested all of his money into one company, United Copper. He believed it was destined for amazing things. He went all in. The company, however, was being targeted by two brothers for what is called a "short squeeze". This is where someone buys stocks heavily, driving the price up in the hope that other traders with short positions (trades that lose money when the price goes up) would rush to close out their positions, which drives the price up further. The scheme failed though and the share price of $30, which pumped up to $60, quickly tanked to $10 and everyone involved lost a huge amount of money.

When the company's stock price collapsed, Edwin Lefevre lost everything. He had a single point of failure and it failed.

If you had invested in purely tech stocks in the 1990s during the dot-com bubble, you would have suffered huge losses when the bubble burst in 2000. If you had all your money in the financial sector pre-2008, you would have been really hurt when the global crisis hit.

As you know, I can't advise you where to invest but I can tell you that it is essential to invest in a variety of things to spread your risk as much as possible.

I personally invest in property, businesses that match my interests or growth plans for my group of businesses, funds, stocks, NFTs, crypto, forex (trading), jewellery and watches. A really widespread set of asset classes. That has taken me years to build up and I continue to build on this all of the time. In fact, as I was sitting writing this chapter my phone buzzed and I have received dividends from my shares in some stocks in the mining sector and I have re-invested that back into shares in the tech sector. I am constantly trying to diversify as much as I can. I will never get it right every time, but if I get it right most of the time, with a diversified portfolio then I am safe from losing everything.

You can take our risk profile quiz to find out your risk profile if you aren't sure. It is over on the website www.sarahpoynton. com/moneymechanicresources

With all risk comes reward! It is that reward that we are seeking. Your potential return on investment is your reward. There is a possibility you could lose money but the trade-off means that you can take advantage of the increase in the value of your investments when it goes right. I say to my clients all the time, it could just as easily go right as it could go wrong! Often, there is a money mindset block here so you have to be open to things going well and that trade-off becomes easier to handle.

The risk-reward trade-off is the relationship between the two. Higher levels of risk usually involve higher levels of reward and lower levels of risk offer lower levels of reward. It makes sense, doesn't it?

As a Money Mechanic, you have to accept the levels of risk when you move forward with any decision, and so understanding the levels of risk you are ok with is going to help you develop.

I personally handle this in a really simple way. I make sure that I never invest what I can't afford to lose, relative to the risk levels.

So, for example, I have some money in a very, very high-risk foreign exchange fund. It is 100% risk in exchange for 30% per month. I have a tiny amount of money in here because the truth is, at a split second's notice, the whole lot could be gone. None is ring-fenced, it is crazy high risk but if it goes well, it will return crazy high rewards. On a pot of £1,000, that is £300 a month. I only need it to go well for 3.33 months, then I can remove my initial capital and this pot can go up and down forever while I have peace of mind that I haven't actually lost anything if it was to all be lost. However, I would never put my FYM fund here because it is possible I could lose it all. My FYM fund is in a low risk reliable, vanilla portfolio.

The money you are relying on, your FYM fund, that money must be invested at a risk level that you are comfortable with. My FYM is invested at around 10 - 15% a year. I am happy with that. Most of my FYM fund is invested at a risk level of around 10%. 90% of my money is protected at all times. I am ok with possibly losing 10% in exchange for the reward but I couldn't handle it if I lost all that money, no way. It would screw everything up, so I would never take big risks with it. That is my future and my freedom.

Investing in stocks carries a higher risk than investing in Bonds, but is likely to offer up higher rewards. Investing in a start-up carries higher risks than investing in a well-established company, but is likely to offer increased rewards.

What you will want to do is strike a balance according to your own goals and risk tolerances. There isn't one single way and this is really personal, so while other people are out there shouting about giant returns for taking big risks, don't get swept up in the hype if you are someone that is happy with the slow and steady.

While the world seems to be obsessed with getting rich quickly, there is absolutely nothing wrong with getting rich slowly. In fact, in most (not all) cases, it is more sustainable and long-lasting.

Use diversification to balance your risk. If you want to do as I do and "play with" a little pot that offers crazy high returns, just to see what happens, then do it, but don't do it with money that is for buying your home, retiring on, paying for your wedding, sending your kids to private school or travelling the world for a year. Do it with money that you have built up and are ready to say goodbye to should things not go to plan.

If you want help determining your risk profile, there is a calculator here www.sarahpoynton.com/moneymechanicsresources or you can connect with qualified financial advisors who can help you establish where you are on the scale and then offer personalised advice.

I used to think I needed to be rich before I spoke to a financial advisor. This is your green light to speak to someone now, even if you are just getting started because they can help you avoid mistakes and tailor your investment plans for your future.

The next really important aspect of risk management is monitoring your investment performance. For some of you, this might be where you are tempted to give up and say it's too much because who has the time to look at all those squiggly lines and numbers and really track things all the time to make sure you don't lose money?

The answer is no one. Unless you are actually a trader for a living, no one has the time to be watching the markets all day, every day, But you don't have to. Most of the platforms I have shared with you in this book have really great tools for measuring performance in the long and short term.

I also have a set time to go through a process of measuring performance at month end. I have businesses, so it is common practice to have a 'month end' review in all my businesses to look at what has happened - money in, money out, the good the bad and the ugly - and I began doing this in my personal world a few years back.

On the last day of the month, I update my net worth tracker and fill it in with all of the values of my portfolios so I can see the trends and ups and downs as I move through the year. I can also see the bigger picture of how all my small revenue streams are impacting my total net worth.

You can download a net worth template tracker on www. sarahpoynton.com/moneymechanicsresources

Money Mechanics like us periodically review their investment portfolios and adjust their investments accordingly. For example, today I saw that my Easyjet stocks have increased by 30% in value since I purchased them. That is an incredible return and so I have opted to sell them while I am up and take that 30% margin, reinvest that into the S&P 500 and then the initial capital I will use to find another stock that I feel looks as though it will perform as well. If I didn't look at these on a regular basis, I may have missed that and whilst I probably wouldn't have lost money, I would have missed an opportunity. These were in my

Freetrade account and it took three clicks on my phone screen to exit those stocks and realise my profit.

I don't do this daily, I am not a trader. I do look at this monthly to just make sure I am on top of the overall performance of my portfolio. In the same regard, if something is underperforming or no longer aligns with my goals or risk tolerance then they have to go in order to rebalance my overall risk and maximise returns.

Another big part of risk management is keeping your emotions under control. Your ego and your fear will play a huge part in your ability to be a good Money Mechanic. This has an official name. It is called "behavioural finance". Behavioural finance is a study that suggests that rather than making rational decisions when it comes to money, people instead make their financial decisions based on emotions and cognitive biases.

Some investors hold onto losing positions for too long, instead of feeling the pain of actually taking the finite loss. There is a global instinct to move with the herd, so most people buy in a bull (rising) market and sell in a bear (decreasing) market. Understanding the psychology behind your decisions can influence your financial decision-making in a really positive way and you can avoid many common pitfalls.

Let's discuss fear first. The presence of fear can overshadow even the most radiant of days. It can lead you to make knee-jerk decisions from a very emotional place. The most common is selling stocks in a market downturn. So many people panic and sell everything to get out quickly because they are worried that they will be left with nothing. The only way you lose is if you sell or the company goes totally bust. The value of the stocks may have gone right down but for as long as you own them, you have not crystalised any loss. It is only when you actually sell that you lose the money. Selling from a place of panic is the quickest way to reduce your wealth. A well-diversified portfolio and a crystal clear investment plan for the long term will help you take the emotion out of your decisions.

Greed is the next influence you must get under control. You know when you eat too many pieces of birthday cake and the only possible outcome is feeling sick... and then a sense of regret as you add up the calories and realise you have to run 900 miles (slight exaggeration maybe) to counter the excessive consumption? Greed when investing will lead you to take on excessive risk. You might start to see 30% a month and think this is great, you put more in, and more in, and more. But greed is likely to push your balanced portfolio out of kilter. If it goes west, you lose more than you were comfortable losing and you have to go back to square one. Overconfidence and over-evaluation of investments are never a good thing. It is like a mirage. To avoid greed rearing its ugly head in your world, focus on being disciplined and crystal clear about your long-term objectives. Don't deviate. Remember, it is ok to get rich slowly. Rely on the data rather than intuition or past success. Success is a shitty teacher. It gives you false confidence in the future and the future simply can't be guaranteed by past performance.

Excitement and anxiety impact your risk management as well. Anxiety will stop you from moving forwards, excitement may make you move forward faster than you are truly comfortable with. A level head is what you must endeavour to cultivate. I was stung by this in my earlier days. I heard a load of hype about a digital currency called Shib in October 2021. I went against all of the rules that I know now and I bought 11,068,712 Shib coins. Yep, you read that right 11 million of the fucking things! I paid around £500, I think. I did almost no due diligence, I just bought because everyone I knew was and I was getting FOMO! The current value of these 11+ million coins is £97. FOMO is a surefire way to lose a load of cash! Had I done my due diligence, I would have seen the trend was at its peak and actually on its way down. Lesson learned. A lesson I learned with £500. Imagine if I had been greedy, as well as excited, and put £5,000 or £50,000 in.

I would be really unhappy now.

I can dream that SHIB will rally one day and I often say to my husband "All I want for Christmas is for SHIB to go to $1 a coin". That would make me very happy. But until it does, I am going to learn from my rookie error and never do that again!

Maintain a level head. Do your due diligence. It is the only way to make the right decisions. Avoid the influence of emotions and stick to your long-term plans instead of getting influenced by your ego or other people's opinions. Ask yourself if you are making this decision from an emotional place, fear, FOMO, anxiety, anger, frustration or greed. Or are you making this decision from a rational, well-thought-through place?

When you ask yourself and you are honest with yourself, you will know the answer!

There are more risk measurement strategies. In my opinion, they are complex and if you are someone that wants to research more about this then you can look into the following:

- Standard deviation
- Value-at-Risk (VaR)
- Conditional Value-at-Risk (CVaR)

However, if you are like me and you want to keep life as simple as possible then remember these rules:

1. Money Mechanics never put all their eggs in one basket

2. Money Mechanics do not make emotional decisions
3. Money Mechanics are in this for the long game and do not panic sell
4. Money Mechanics diversify as much as they can

Stick to those four rules and you will strike a pretty solid balance between risk and reward.

When you do that, you will be able to maintain your financial growth long into the future!

CHAPTER 12

DIVERSIFIED PATHWAYS: NAVIGATING THE TERRAIN OF ALTERNATIVE INVESTMENTS

O K, all the way through this book, I promised to make sure I only spoke about things I know about from experience.

This is a bit of a bonus chapter to share some ideas and to clear up any confusion about some of these asset classes. I want to say straight out of the gate, that I have been doing everything else in this book for years. Forex, Crypto, Booze, Art etc. are all reasonably new on my radar and as I have said throughout the book, I am not advising you at all, I am simply sharing what I have learned to set your brain matter off thinking. I want to open the door of possibility for you to walk through and carry out your own due diligence.

Why would anyone want to look at investing in these types of asset classes?

Well, in my mind, diversification is key but by opening up to different types of asset classes, you can invest in some things that are really interesting to you.

Since school, I have always had a secret love for Picasso. I had to recreate a piece of work by him for an art class once and my hyper-focus tendencies kicked in on this project and I took a deep dive into all his works. It blows my mind and I love it. It isn't for everyone but I just love it. A slightly off-topic fun fact - did you know Picasso died in 1971? Until I studied him, I thought he lived in the 17th Century and his art was really really old. It isn't. My favourite is probably "Le Rêve", the painting of Marie-Thérèse. It is a distorted depiction of her, using contrasting colours and simple outlines. It was sold in 1941 for $7000 and in 1997, it sold again for $48.4 million. In fifty-six years it increased in value by 691,329%, which is an average of 12,345% a year.

Now, I am working on my pot of $48.4 million + to be able to buy myself the original "Le Rêve" (a girl can dream right?). While I am doing that, I can see that there are plenty of other channels to acquire amazing art. It won't all see this level of increase in value but even the unknowns are often increasing in value by a huge amount, year-on-year. And when you look at the statistics, Art outperforms the markets and holds a very special resilience to economic downturns. In 2021, the Art Basel and US Global Art Market Report said that the art market's total value was estimated at $50.1 billion, up 7% from 2019, demonstrating that art seems to be very resilient through tough times. We all know what was happening in 2020 and 2021, don't we?

When you combine this resilience with low volatility and a limited supply, it makes a solid strategy for investment. And art is also very tangible. For those of you that want to enjoy your investments, art could well be a route to go. I have no idea what to suggest is a good artist to invest in (apart from Picasso, obviously) but if it is something you have ever considered, I wanted you to know you aren't mad - the numbers and the trends present art to be a very solid way to build wealth.

Let's talk about booze. If you are someone that can be trusted not to drink it, then fine wine, whiskey, craft beer and some spirits can be excellent investments. Alcohol is an alternative investment but a lucrative one. My father-in-law has limited-edition whiskeys that have doubled in price in just a few years. Knight Frank Luxury Investment Index, which tracks the price growth of ten luxury asset classes, reports that rare whiskey has increased by 564% since 2010.

Likewise, craft beer has seen a recent surge in popularity and is considered by the industry to be an emerging asset class for investment. Now the purists argue with this, but the purists also said in 1966 that online shopping would be a "total failure". People are frightened of what they don't understand, but it doesn't mean that it won't take off.

Which segues very nicely to cryptocurrency.

Right now, we are in the early adopters/early majority phases of cryptocurrency. Most people have heard of it but the masses still believe it to be dodgy, unnecessary or simply something that nerds do. Most people are frightened of it because they simply don't understand it. Now, I am not an expert in crypto but I am investing time and effort into improving my knowledge in this space.

Here is my take on it.

Cryptocurrency is a digital or virtual currency. It uses cryptography for security and is decentralised. That means there isn't a central authority that controls it. The dollar is centralised by the Federal Reserve System. The pound is centralised by the Bank of England. Cryptocurrency doesn't have a central control like Fiat (the currency you and I use every day) currency has.

Cryptocurrency uses blockchain technology. If you imagine a chain, like a metal chain that you would use to close a gate, the chain links all connect and it is the combination of the links all together that give substance to the chain. If you removed a link, the chain would break and it wouldn't be any good. The blockchain is similar. It is made up of blocks that are linked together in a sequential and unalterable manner. Each block contains a set of transactions that have been verified and recorded. Once a block has been added, it cannot be changed or deleted without altering the whole chain, which is why it is so secure. It is a ledger system that records everything in an unalterable way, which maintains security and transparency.

Bitcoin is probably the most well-known cryptocurrency in the world today. It was created in 2009 by an anonymous individual (or group of individuals). They used the pseudonym of Satoshi Nakamoto. Ever since then, thousands of new currencies have been created and these are known as Altcoins (alternative coins). The most well-known of these are Ethereum and Ripple, but this is changing all the time. In fact, by the time you read this, there will probably have been hundreds of new altcoins introduced into the market.

Now, I do not fully understand (or want to understand) the inner workings of how cryptocurrency tech works. All I really care about, as a Money Mechanic, is whether investing in or holding cryptocurrency is a good or bad idea in relation to my own targets and risk profile.

What do we know for sure?

We know that in the UK, the USA and other countries, our governments are regularly "printing" money and adding an additional supply of money into circulation. What this means is that the value of that money goes down. In simple terms, the more they add, the more there is, and so the more the value of it reduces.

The thing about crypto that people like is that there is a finite volume of each currency available, which means it will retain intrinsic value over time. Arguably, as more and more people get involved in holding and using crypto, the value will increase because the supply is reducing and demand is increasing.

There are only 21 million bitcoins available and there will only ever be 21 million available. If you allow me to hypothesise for a minute, imagine fifty years from now, if the world moves towards cryptocurrencies, which the current trends would suggest we are going to do. With a finite number available, those that hold Bitcoin will be able to buy things and those without Bitcoin won't, which will make the financial divide even more vast than it is now. This feels like a stretch right now but again, in 1966 online shopping felt like a stretch and look where we are just fifty-seven years later.

The early adopters bought cryptocurrency very cheaply from 2009 onwards and actually, many have become multi-millionaires because they moved fast. However, many of them are not selling because the long play is to actually have cryptocurrency that can be used to pay for things now and in the future. It is unlikely the crypto values will move upward at the same pace they have since 2009 but who really knows? If banks collapse, and Fiat currency becomes worthless, then crypto may well see vast increases in value. This is an extreme outcome but we never know what is coming our way, do we? That is one thing that 2020 and 2021 taught us, if nothing else. None of us has a crystal ball and I hope this triggers your research into this space.

The thing I love about crypto that you probably don't know is that you can use it to buy normal things - normal, everyday things like petrol, coffee, bills, food, things for the house, vet bills; everything. I have a VISA card (which most of you will recognise) but instead of there being pounds on it, it is loaded with cryptocurrency, and when I spend on it, I get cashback on the money I am spending in crypto, so it is reloading my card for me with money to spend. I told you all about this in the rewards chapter. I use crypto.com for this. My link is https://crypto.com/app/c6zhusnamx and when I stake (which means lock-in) £3,000 on the card, I get cash back on my spending and my Spotify and Netflix subscription gives me 100% cashback.

When I first got involved with this card, I staked £3,000 for 90 days and in those 90 days, my £3,000 increased in value to £9,000. I took £6,000 out and left £3,000 in. Taking my initial capital back, plus I pulled my initial capital out to invest in something else and I am left with £3,000 of free money that is now in the account and it will go up and down with the market without me worrying about it.

Whatever that money does now, or ten years from now, it is an infinite return because I have had all my initial invested money back out. I see this as one of the best ways to mitigate risk. To always be working your initial capital out and then letting the profits work forever.

Crypto might be something you have heard loads about and something that you are actually frightened of because you don't understand it, but if you want my 10p worth, I think it is important for everyone to understand this more and to start considering how it could work for them. Do not jump in without due diligence, and never invest what you can't afford to lose - you know the rules by now - but I really think it is important to open yourself up and entertain the idea of having crypto in your world in order to prepare for the future.

Let's talk about trading forex now. I have a love-hate relationship with this form of investing and I will tell you why in a second. First, though, let me explain what Forex is.

If you have ever been abroad and traded your currency for another country's currency then you have traded the foreign exchange market without even realising it.

When you use Pounds to buy Dollars, or you use Euros to buy Chinese Yen, you are trading the foreign exchange markets. Almost all of us have done it at least once.

The foreign exchange market is estimated to have an average trading volume of $6.6 trillion per day, which makes it the largest financial market in the world. Not that that really matters to you in the day-to-day. What matters to you is that there are ways that you can make money from investing or trading this market.

Now, I am no trader. I am neither patient enough nor am I emotionally intelligent enough to be a trader. I am ok with that. What I do instead is invest my money into forex funds that are run by fund managers in an active way and they do the trading with my money and I either earn a profit or make a loss on their performance.

I am writing this in the middle of a week where I have seen a £6,000 loss on one of my forex funds. That is the truth and I promised you at the start of this book that I would share the ups and downs of putting your money to work. This is by far and away the riskiest investment I am involved with, but also the one that returns the most money, the fastest, when it is going well. To balance out the story of that loss, that same fund has generated around 30% a month on the total amount in the account for months prior to this loss, so my initial capital hasn't been lost because I have cycled the profits out as I was making them. They have gone into other things. I knew the risk was high, but a loss is still a loss and it hurts when it happens.

I will remain in the forex market though because I know that actually, across the landscape of my investments over a year, I am up. The lesson here is that you must do your due diligence on any fund that you invest in and you must never, ever invest what you can't afford to lose in these incredibly high-risk opportunities.

Instead, you can find forex funds that have really tight risk management measures. I am in one forex fund that ring-fences 90% of my money, so only 10% is at risk at any one time and that is performing really well at around 12-15% per year with a minimum investment of just £2,000. You can find forex trading funds that match your personal risk profile, you don't have to risk big to benefit from the forex market. Proceed with caution though, you have been warned!

All of the Money Mechanic vehicles I have mentioned in this chapter are either misunderstood or create fear in people because they are so far removed from what they know. What I hope this chapter has done is open up your mind to something that you could start to look into. If I can help at all then come and talk to me over on Instagram @moneymechanics.global. I can't give you advice but I can certainly talk to you about my experiences - the good, the bad, the expensive and the profitable!

CHAPTER 13

FINANCIAL LEVERAGE: RISKY BUSINESS OR WINNING STRATEGY?

You have learned about compound interest, leverage is the next hack that you can take advantage of as a Money Mechanic.

In the world of money, leverage refers to the use of borrowed capital (money) to increase the potential return on your investment. In simple terms, you use other people's money. This can be done in various ways but loans are the most common. This is the most common form of leverage that I use in my business to create wealth faster.

Leverage allows you to amplify your gains by risking less of your own money. You put in a smaller amount to control a larger amount of assets than would be possible with your own money. Or you put in the same amount of money but you can spread that amount over a wider range of assets which helps you to mitigate risk through diversification. There are risks associated with leverage and the misuse of leverage can have catastrophic consequences at an institutional level, as we saw happen in 2008. It was a big contributing factor to the global economic crisis of that year. Much of the issue was that institutional investors were borrowing money to invest and when they lost, they lost the borrowed money, which had a huge knock-on effect on the wider world. It was like a house of cards that tumbled as borrowers at every level defaulted on loans that they couldn't afford to repay.

Anyone reading this that has ever bought a house and used a mortgage to do it, has used leverage. Leverage is really common in the business world. We all know that companies take loans or investments and they use that investment to build revenue and ultimately profits, but it is less known in the personal finance world. Mortgages are where this happens the most. You take on debt to be able to buy a property. When it is your own home, the goal is not always to create a quick profit. Instead we are happy to leverage to create an increase in value over time.

Imagine you invest in property and real estate. You find something that is being sold for £100,000. You take out a residential mortgage for 90% of that (which is available in the market at the time of writing this). You have borrowed £90,000 and you put in £10,000 of your own money. In this case, you are leveraging other people's money to control a more valuable asset.

Let's say the property value increases by 10% to £110,000. Your initial investment of £10,000 has grown to £20,000 (excluding fees and interest and tax), giving you a 100% return. If you had not leveraged other people's money then the first issue would have been that you wouldn't have had enough money to buy the house in the first place, but let's just play for a second. If you had found a house for £10,000 and it had gone up in value by 10% you would have only made £1,000.

In this example, you also have a higher exposure to risk when you don't leverage other people's money. If the property was to reduce in value by 10% to £90,000 and you sold, you would lose your £10,000 entirely. If you decided to sell at £90,000 you would have the £90,000 loan to repay and so you would be left with no money and no house.

One of the most common ways for people to use leverage to buy property is to buy the property for £100,000 using leverage, a loan of £90,000. Then when the market goes up or you have added value to the property, you sell. Let's say it goes up by 10%, you sell for £110,000. You pay back your loan of £90,000 and you are left with £20,000.

This example is for demo purposes only and you would need to do the numbers properly to know the cost of borrowing and buying and how those fees and interest rates and tax etc. impact the profits, but for the purpose of this chapter, I wanted to give you an example of how you can use other people's money to create wealth through property in a far more efficient way than trying to save up all the money you need to buy a property with cash.

Where this becomes really sexy and something that we do in our property business regularly is where we work with people who invest in our business in exchange for interest on the loan and we use that money to create homes (buying houses). Let me explain a bit more.

Let's say that someone has a pot of £50,000 or £100,000 (sometimes more) sitting in the bank. As we have already discussed in this book, they are probably getting very, very low interest on those savings. Even with a rapid increase in interest rates on borrowing in 2023, savers are still not seeing those rates reflected in their accounts which means their money is eroding every day thanks to inflation.

The way we work with those people is to help facilitate them to put their money to work. We borrow their money, in the same way we would borrow mortgage money from a bank, but instead of paying the interest to the bank, we pay the same interest to those investors. We still do the same thing with those funds - we buy a property, we add value and we either sell it or rent it out, but instead of working with a bank, we work with individuals or smaller businesses.

Let me give you a real-life example to make this tangible for you so you can see how you too could take advantage of this in the real world.

I purchased a house for £102,000 with my business partners. It was a three-bedroom terrace property. The lady that lived in it had sadly passed away and her children were selling it to realise their inheritance. When the daughter approached us, she told us they were looking for £102,000 but the property needed a huge amount of work. It hadn't been decorated or really any maintenance done on the property in around forty years, so you can imagine what it was like. The lady that had lived there had smoked and so we lovingly nicknamed this house nicotine towers because the walls and ceilings were yellow!

What we knew was that if this property was newly renovated, it would likely sell for around £190,000.

We could buy it for £102,000.

We could spend around £50,000 on the work.

We would spend around £10,000 on fees and charges.

This left us with a £28,000 profit once we completed and sold the project.

But we didn't have the £50,000 to do the work. So instead, I connected with a business owner on Facebook that had £50,000 and she wanted to invest this for a fixed return. We agreed to pay her a fixed rate that was higher than what she was getting in the bank. That meant that we could do a project that we wouldn't have been able to do without leveraging her company's money.

So, we put in 25% of the £102,000.

We used the investors' loan of £50,000 to add value to the property.

We spent £10,000 on fees and charges.

Once the project was completed it was actually valued at £200,000.

Once it was sold, we paid back the £50,000 loan, we paid her the interest, we paid back 75% loan to the bank of £76,500, our £25,000 deposit and our £10,000 in fees which left us with a £30,000+ profit. We initially put in £35,000 of our money to make that. Once completed, that left a pot of £68,500 instead of £35,000 and that took around twelve months to complete. That project would simply have not been possible for us had we not used other people's money. The £76,500 from the bank and £50,000 from the investor.

The bank is happy because they earned fees and interest on their money.

The investor is happy because they have earned more money on their £50,000 than they were getting in the bank

We were happy because we were able to transact and create a brand new home for a family and also create a profit.

This sort of leverage is available to everyone. Of course, you have to understand how it works, and you have to build connections with people you could work with. Ultimately though, there is power in leverage. It allows you to fast-track what is possible in a short space of time.

There is, of course, compliance and legislation that surrounds this way of taking on investment to protect people who have savings and want to invest in companies like mine. That legislation is there to protect you and whether you are looking to take on investment or lend as an investor, you really should do some due diligence on the rules that surround this. Do not just jump into anything like this without doing your research first. If I can help at all, get in touch with me at www.sarahpoynton.com/moneymechanicsresources

I would also give you a word of warning that if you do decide to become an investor and let someone else leverage your money in exchange for a hands-off interest income, then do not put all your eggs in one basket. Do not hand over your life savings. Remember, Money Mechanics always diversify and we always do our research. There is always going to be a risk, and you will never mitigate against everything. I see so many cases where people jump into bed with new contacts, excited by all the upside, and their savings are destroyed because they put everything they had into one place. Don't do that!

This chapter wasn't really supposed to terrify you. It is supposed to inspire you to open up your mind to the options that you have. Using other people's money to grow your wealth is something you have available to you right now. You simply have to learn how.

You could take advantage of margin trading. I don't do this personally; it sits outside of my risk profile. You may have guessed by now I am not a naturally big risk-taker. Margin trading is where you borrow money to invest in securities like stocks or bonds. Because you are borrowing money, it allows you to buy more of the security than you would be able to do yourself. It's similar to using a mortgage to buy property but for a different space in the market. With property, the bricks are the collateral for the loan, and with margin trading, the securities (shares) are the collateral.

Here are the numbers to make it tangible:

Let's say you have £5,000 to invest and want to buy shares of a company. Without margin trading, you could buy 100 shares at £50 per share. Now, suppose you decided to leverage a broker's money that was offering a 2:1 margin. This means for every £1 you invest, they will lend you another £1. You could now buy 200 shares of the same company at £50 a share. If the price goes up to £60 a share, your investment would now be worth £12,000. After you paid back the borrowed £5,000 and your initial £5,000, you would have a profit of £2,000.

That said if the stock price dropped to £40 your investment would now be worth £8,000. After you paid back the leveraged money of £5,000, you would be left with £3,000, losing £2,000 of your initial investment.

In principle, you are simply borrowing money to make money. That is the basis of leverage in whatever capacity you choose to apply it.

If I can help you understand this in more detail then please get in touch with me. I work with clients regularly who want to learn how to raise private finance for their businesses. Since I started out doing this, I have personally been involved in raising over

£5,000,000 of private finance for my business and my clients, and I have many clients that I have taught to do this who have raised millions of pounds as well. It works like a dream when you get it right but you have to be sure you are doing it properly, compliantly and with risk factored in at every stage!

CHAPTER 14
REDEFINING WEALTH: TURNING FINANCIAL LITERACY INTO ACTION

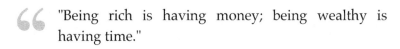 "Being rich is having money; being wealthy is having time."

MARGARET BONNANO

Financial independence doesn't come from simply working more and earning more. It comes from learning how to produce more from what you have. It comes from you having the understanding that you will never be able to out-earn a spending problem. And realising that whenever we spend money on pointless things instead of investing it, we are actually stealing from our future selves. We are stealing the time it took to produce the money but also the future freedom that it will give us.

Stop fucking with the future you! They won't appreciate it!

If the methods you have been using up until now are not working, then now is the time to activate change. Financial independence is not a pipe dream, it can be a reality for us all. It is going to be tough, and you are going to have to evolve into a new version of yourself. I talked at the beginning of the book about your money mindset. Now is the time to let go of anything that is no longer serving you. The new version of you cannot carry the same burdens into financial independence or your freeze, fight or flight will kick in and you will go back to old habits. They say old habits die hard, but if you know that your habits are toxic to your future then it is time to say goodbye to them. Instead, seek out knowledge, be open to new ideas, test things and explore options until you find what works for you. When you eventually let go of what is holding you back, your whole world will spin differently.

The rules I have laid out in this book start by knowing where you are right now, figuring out where you want to be, paying back all of the bad debt that is currently holding you back and then working to build a diversified income-generating portfolio of investments.

Seems simple when I say it like that, doesn't it?

Investments will allow you to earn money whether you get up and go to work or not. You will earn money while you sleep. I am not saying live a life of doing and having nothing for years so you can enjoy life later. Tomorrow isn't promised and so you must strike a balance. What I am saying to you is that when you develop the discipline to budget and stick to a plan of putting a percentage of your money each month towards your future freedom, then you really can have it all. By paying into your future you are ensuring a future for yourself with less money worries, more choice and early retirement if that is what you want.

Financial independence doesn't come from having millions and millions. If it did then there wouldn't be high-net-worth people worrying about money, but there most certainly are. Financial independence comes from choosing to do the best you can with what you have. When you follow the Money Mechanics rules, you will be able to create a life that is the life that you choose for yourself.

Forget how other people are doing life, focus on YOU.

It all starts with just one step towards something different.

£1 overpaid each week towards a credit card.

£1 added to an Index fund each week.

£1 a week overpaid on your residential mortgage.

£1 saved towards your emergency fund.

In the early days, it might feel a little pointless, but that £1 isn't the thing to focus on. It is the action. The discipline to actually do it. That is the thing that matters most. When you move from thinking about doing it to actually doing it, it will be easier to continue doing it. You will build momentum and confidence. As your confidence builds, you can go from £1 to £5 to £50 and over time, that will have a huge impact on your results. Plus, as your confidence builds and you start to see your net worth growing (because you are now tracking it every month), you will be fuelled to do this again and again.

Start today. Don't wait. Time isn't on your side.

£1,000 invested for twenty years at 10% with an additional £100 a month added = £83,264

£1,000 invested for twenty-five years at 10% with an additional £100 a month added = £144,740

Waiting for five years has cost you £61,476 - DON'T WAIT!

You have the rules to follow now, but the rest is up to you. You have to follow the steps and let go of what has not been working for you up until now.

My Grandad taught me years ago that you will always get from life a result that is directly linked to the level of effort you put in. Choose to activate change, mean it and you will start to feel the results. Allow the small wins in the early days to be your fuel. Celebrate your wins along the way.

Cleared a credit card - celebrate!

Bought your first share - celebrate!

Earned your first dividend - celebrate!

You have got this!

I have one last thing to ask of you. I wrote this book because I hope that more people will discover what I have discovered, that earning more money and the pressure that brings actually isn't the answer. Putting the money we have to work is the answer to true financial independence. As you start to see the change in your world, please share this with everyone you know. Let's normalise the conversation about money, debt and investing.

Imagine a world where all our decisions are made from a place of true desire and not from a place of fear of the financial consequences of those decisions.

You are a Money Mechanic now!

Together we can redefine wealth!

Printed in Great Britain
by Amazon